ECM
Complete Self-Assessment Guide

The guidance in this Self-Assessment is based on ECM best practices and standards in business process architecture, design and quality management. The guidance is also based on the professional judgment of the individual collaborators listed in the Acknowledgments.

Notice of rights

Trademarks

Copyright © by The Art of Service
http://theartofservice.com
service@theartofservice.com

Table of Contents

About The Art of Service

The Art of Service, Business Process Architects since 2000, is dedicated to helping stakeholders achieve excellence.

Defining, designing, creating, and implementing a process to solve a stakeholders challenge or meet an objective is the most valuable role… In EVERY group, company, organization and department.

Unless you're talking a one-time, single-use project, there should be a process. Whether that process is managed and implemented by humans, AI, or a combination of the two, it needs to be designed by someone with a complex enough perspective to ask the right questions.

Someone capable of asking the right questions and step back and say, 'What are we really trying to accomplish here? And is there a different way to look at it?'

With The Art of Service's Standard Requirements Self-Assessments, we empower people who can do just that — whether their title is marketer, entrepreneur, manager, salesperson, consultant, Business Process Manager, executive assistant, IT Manager, CIO etc... —they are the people who rule the future. They are people who watch the process as it happens, and ask the right questions to make the process work better.

Contact us when you need any support with this Self-Assessment and any help with templates, blue-prints and examples of standard documents you might need:

http://theartofservice.com
service@theartofservice.com

Acknowledgments

This checklist was developed under the auspices of The Art of Service, chaired by Gerardus Blokdyk.

Representatives from several client companies participated in the preparation of this Self-Assessment.

In addition, we are thankful for the design and printing services provided.

Included Resources - how to access

Included with your purchase of the book is the ECM Self-Assessment Spreadsheet Dashboard which contains all questions and Self-Assessment areas and auto-generates insights, graphs, and project RACI planning - all with examples to get you started right away.

How? Simply send an email to
access@theartofservice.com
with this books' title in the subject to get the ECM Self Assessment Tool right away.

You will receive the following contents with New and Updated specific criteria:

• The latest quick edition of the book in PDF

• The latest complete edition of the book in PDF, which criteria correspond to the criteria in...

• The Self-Assessment Excel Dashboard, and...

• Example pre-filled Self-Assessment Excel Dashboard to get familiar with results generation

• In-depth specific Checklists covering the topic

• Project management checklists and templates to assist with implementation

INCLUDES LIFETIME SELF ASSESSMENT UPDATES

Every self assessment comes with Lifetime Updates and Lifetime Free Updated Books. Lifetime Updates is an industry-first feature which allows you to receive verified self assessment updates, ensuring you always have the most accurate information at your fingertips.

Get it now- you will be glad you did - do it now, before you forget.

Send an email to **access@theartofservice.com** with this books' title in the subject to get the ECM Self Assessment Tool right away.

Your feedback is invaluable to us

If you recently bought this book, we would love to hear from you! You can do this by writing a review on amazon (or the online store where you purchased this book) about your last purchase! As part of our continual service improvement process, we love to hear real client experiences and feedback.

How does it work?
To post a review on Amazon, just log in to your account and click on the Create Your Own Review button (under Customer Reviews) of the relevant product page. You can find examples of product reviews in Amazon. If you purchased from another online store, simply follow their procedures.

What happens when I submit my review?
Once you have submitted your review, send us an email at review@theartofservice.com with the link to your review so we can properly thank you for your feedback.

Purpose of this Self-Assessment

This Self-Assessment has been developed to improve understanding of the requirements and elements of ECM, based on best practices and standards in business process architecture, design and quality management.

It is designed to allow for a rapid Self-Assessment to determine how closely existing management practices and procedures correspond to the elements of the Self-Assessment.

The criteria of requirements and elements of ECM have been rephrased in the format of a Self-Assessment questionnaire, with a seven-criterion scoring system, as explained in this document.

In this format, even with limited background knowledge of ECM, a manager can quickly review existing operations to determine how they measure up to the standards. This in turn can serve as the starting point of a 'gap analysis' to identify management tools or system elements that might usefully be implemented in the organization to help improve overall performance.

How to use the Self-Assessment

On the following pages are a series of questions to identify to what extent your ECM initiative is complete in comparison to the requirements set in standards.

To facilitate answering the questions, there is a space in front of each question to enter a score on a scale of '1' to '5'.

1 Strongly Disagree

2 Disagree

3 Neutral

4 Agree

5 Strongly Agree

Read the question and rate it with the following in front of mind:

**'In my belief,
the answer to this question is clearly defined'.**

There are two ways in which you can choose to interpret this statement;
1. how aware are you that the answer to the question is clearly defined
2. for more in-depth analysis you can choose to gather evidence and confirm the answer to the question. This obviously will take more time, most Self-Assessment

users opt for the first way to interpret the question and dig deeper later on based on the outcome of the overall Self-Assessment.

A score of '1' would mean that the answer is not clear at all, where a '5' would mean the answer is crystal clear and defined. Leave emtpy when the question is not applicable or you don't want to answer it, you can skip it without affecting your score. Write your score in the space provided.

After you have responded to all the appropriate statements in each section, compute your average score for that section, using the formula provided, and round to the nearest tenth. Then transfer to the corresponding spoke in the ECM Scorecard on the second next page of the Self-Assessment.

Your completed ECM Scorecard will give you a clear presentation of which ECM areas need attention.

ECM
Scorecard Example

Example of how the finalized Scorecard can look like:

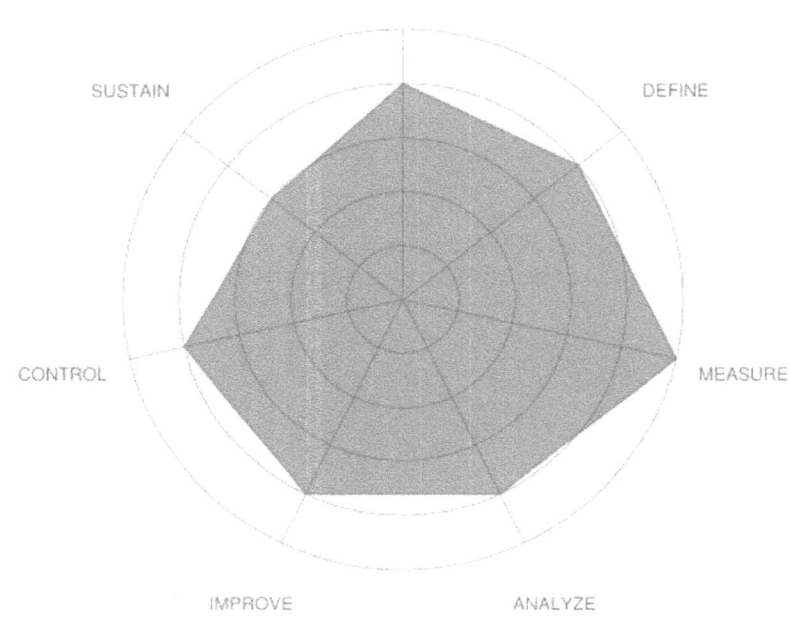

ECM
Scorecard

Your Scores:

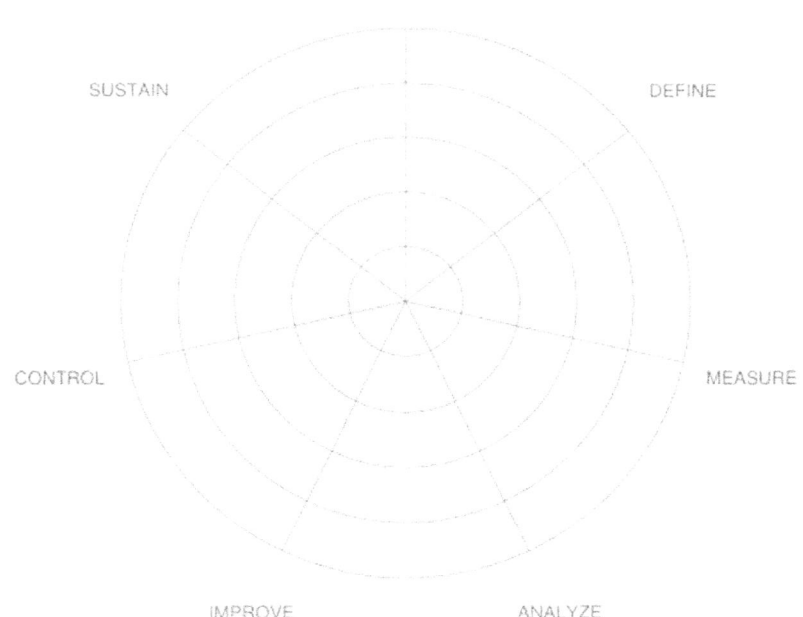

BEGINNING OF THE SELF-ASSESSMENT:

CRITERION #1: RECOGNIZE

INTENT: Be aware of the need for change. Recognize that there is an unfavorable variation, problem or symptom.

In my belief, the answer to this question is clearly defined:

5 Strongly Agree

4 Agree

3 Neutral

2 Disagree

1 Strongly Disagree

1. Are controls defined to recognize and contain problems?
<--- Score

2. Do your E-forms support the need to retain the look and feel of paper forms?
<--- Score

3. What does ECM success mean to the stakeholders?

<--- Score

4. Who else hopes to benefit from it?
<--- Score

5. What are your needs in relation to ECM skills, labor, equipment, and markets?
<--- Score

6. What tools and technologies are needed for a custom ECM project?
<--- Score

7. When a ECM manager recognizes a problem, what options are available?
<--- Score

8. Does ECM create potential expectations in other areas that need to be recognized and considered?
<--- Score

9. Who defines the rules in relation to any given issue?
<--- Score

10. Do you know what you need to know about ECM?
<--- Score

11. Can management personnel recognize the monetary benefit of ECM?
<--- Score

12. For your ECM project, identify and describe the business environment, is there more than one layer to the business environment?
<--- Score

13. To what extent does each concerned units management team recognize ECM as an effective investment?
<--- Score

14. What needs to be done?
<--- Score

15. Do you need different information or graphics?
<--- Score

16. What problems are you facing and how do you consider ECM will circumvent those obstacles?
<--- Score

17. What situation(s) led to this ECM Self Assessment?
<--- Score

18. Will new equipment/products be required to facilitate ECM delivery, for example is new software needed?
<--- Score

19. Consider your own ECM project, what types of organizational problems do you think might be causing or affecting your problem, based on the work done so far?
<--- Score

20. Are your goals realistic? Do you need to redefine your problem? Perhaps the problem has changed or maybe you have reached your goal and need to set a new one?
<--- Score

21. Why Do you Need AECMA SE?

<--- Score

22. How do you assess your ECM workforce capability and capacity needs, including skills, competencies, and staffing levels?
<--- Score

23. What information do users need?
<--- Score

24. Is it clear when you think of the day ahead of you what activities and tasks you need to complete?
<--- Score

25. How do you identify the kinds of information that you will need?
<--- Score

26. Does your organization need more ECM education?
<--- Score

27. What are the minority interests and what amount of minority interests can be recognized?
<--- Score

28. What should be considered when identifying available resources, constraints, and deadlines?
<--- Score

29. Looking at each person individually – does every one have the qualities which are needed to work in this group?
<--- Score

30. Are there any specific expectations or concerns

about the ECM team, ECM itself?
<--- Score

31. How can auditing be a preventative security measure?
<--- Score

32. What do you need to start doing?
<--- Score

33. Will a response program recognize when a crisis occurs and provide some level of response?
<--- Score

34. Will it solve real problems?
<--- Score

35. What is the smallest subset of the problem you can usefully solve?
<--- Score

36. To what extent would your organization benefit from being recognized as a award recipient?
<--- Score

37. How are you going to measure success?
<--- Score

38. Should you invest in industry-recognized qualications?
<--- Score

39. What else needs to be measured?
<--- Score

40. Will ECM deliverables need to be tested and, if so,

by whom?
<--- Score

41. Who needs what information?
<--- Score

42. Are there ECM problems defined?
<--- Score

43. Who are your key stakeholders who need to sign off?
<--- Score

44. What are the business objectives to be achieved with ECM?
<--- Score

45. Who had the original idea?
<--- Score

46. What prevents you from making the changes you know will make you a more effective ECM leader?
<--- Score

47. How does it fit into your organizational needs and tasks?
<--- Score

48. How much are sponsors, customers, partners, stakeholders involved in ECM? In other words, what are the risks, if ECM does not deliver successfully?
<--- Score

49. What vendors make products that address the ECM needs?
<--- Score

50. What are the expected benefits of ECM to the business?
<--- Score

51. What would happen if ECM weren't done?
<--- Score

52. Are you dealing with any of the same issues today as yesterday? What can you do about this?
<--- Score

53. How do you take a forward-looking perspective in identifying ECM research related to market response and models?
<--- Score

54. Do you have/need 24-hour access to key personnel?
<--- Score

55. As a sponsor, customer or management, how important is it to meet goals, objectives?
<--- Score

56. What are the timeframes required to resolve each of the issues/problems?
<--- Score

57. Think about the people you identified for your ECM project and the project responsibilities you would assign to them. what kind of training do you think they would need to perform these responsibilities effectively?
<--- Score

58. Are problem definition and motivation clearly presented?
<--- Score

59. Are there recognized ECM problems?
<--- Score

60. Do you need to avoid or amend any ECM activities?
<--- Score

61. What is the problem or issue?
<--- Score

62. Who needs to know about ECM?
<--- Score

63. What training and capacity building actions are needed to implement proposed reforms?
<--- Score

64. Are there any revenue recognition issues?
<--- Score

65. What extra resources will you need?
<--- Score

66. How are the ECM's objectives aligned to the organization's overall business strategy?
<--- Score

Add up total points for this section:
_ _ _ _ _ = Total points for this section

Divided by: _ _ _ _ _ _ (number of statements answered) = _ _ _ _ _ _

Average score for this section

Transfer your score to the ECM Index at
the beginning of the Self-Assessment.

CRITERION #2: DEFINE:

INTENT: Formulate the business problem. Define the problem, needs and objectives.

In my belief, the answer to this question is clearly defined:

5 Strongly Agree

4 Agree

3 Neutral

2 Disagree

1 Strongly Disagree

1. Who are the ECM improvement team members, including Management Leads and Coaches?
<--- Score

2. Does the scope remain the same?
<--- Score

3. Has your scope been defined?
<--- Score

4. What is the definition of success?
<--- Score

5. How do you gather ECM requirements?
<--- Score

6. Are there any constraints known that bear on the ability to perform ECM work? How is the team addressing them?
<--- Score

7. What customer feedback methods were used to solicit their input?
<--- Score

8. What specifically is the problem? Where does it occur? When does it occur? What is its extent?
<--- Score

9. Do you all define ECM in the same way?
<--- Score

10. How is the team tracking and documenting its work?
<--- Score

11. How was the 'as is' process map developed, reviewed, verified and validated?
<--- Score

12. How will variation in the actual durations of each activity be dealt with to ensure that the expected ECM results are met?
<--- Score

13. Have the customer needs been translated into specific, measurable requirements? How?
<--- Score

14. What is the scope?
<--- Score

15. What is out-of-scope initially?
<--- Score

16. Is the ECM scope manageable?
<--- Score

17. What happens if ECM's scope changes?
<--- Score

18. Have specific policy objectives been defined?
<--- Score

19. Do the problem and goal statements meet the SMART criteria (specific, measurable, attainable, relevant, and time-bound)?
<--- Score

20. Has/have the customer(s) been identified?
<--- Score

21. Will team members perform ECM work when assigned and in a timely fashion?
<--- Score

22. When are meeting minutes sent out? Who is on the distribution list?
<--- Score

23. What are the compelling business reasons for

embarking on ECM?
<--- Score

24. Are business processes mapped?
<--- Score

25. In what way can you redefine the criteria of choice clients have in your category in your favor?
<--- Score

26. If substitutes have been appointed, have they been briefed on the ECM goals and received regular communications as to the progress to date?
<--- Score

27. Has the improvement team collected the 'voice of the customer' (obtained feedback – qualitative and quantitative)?
<--- Score

28. What is the scope of ECM?
<--- Score

29. Who is gathering ECM information?
<--- Score

30. How often are the team meetings?
<--- Score

31. What was the context?
<--- Score

32. Is the ECM scope complete and appropriately sized?
<--- Score

33. Is the team adequately staffed with the desired cross-functionality? If not, what additional resources are available to the team?
<--- Score

34. Has the direction changed at all during the course of ECM? If so, when did it change and why?
<--- Score

35. What constraints exist that might impact the team?
<--- Score

36. Is it clearly defined in and to your organization what you do?
<--- Score

37. What is in scope?
<--- Score

38. Has a team charter been developed and communicated?
<--- Score

39. Is scope creep really all bad news?
<--- Score

40. What are the tasks and definitions?
<--- Score

41. Is the improvement team aware of the different versions of a process: what they think it is vs. what it actually is vs. what it should be vs. what it could be?
<--- Score

42. What system do you use for gathering ECM

information?
<--- Score

43. Who defines (or who defined) the rules and roles?
<--- Score

44. Is ECM linked to key business goals and objectives?
<--- Score

45. What key business process output measure(s) does ECM leverage and how?
<--- Score

46. What ECM requirements should be gathered?
<--- Score

47. What is out of scope?
<--- Score

48. Does the team have regular meetings?
<--- Score

49. What are the record-keeping requirements of ECM activities?
<--- Score

50. Is ECM currently on schedule according to the plan?
<--- Score

51. What is in the scope and what is not in scope?
<--- Score

52. Are audit criteria, scope, frequency and methods defined?

<--- Score

53. Are customers identified and high impact areas defined?
<--- Score

54. How did the ECM manager receive input to the development of a ECM improvement plan and the estimated completion dates/times of each activity?
<--- Score

55. Are roles and responsibilities formally defined?
<--- Score

56. Has everyone on the team, including the team leaders, been properly trained?
<--- Score

57. What defines best in class?
<--- Score

58. How do you manage scope?
<--- Score

59. Is there a completed SIPOC representation, describing the Suppliers, Inputs, Process, Outputs, and Customers?
<--- Score

60. Is the team sponsored by a champion or business leader?
<--- Score

61. Is a fully trained team formed, supported, and committed to work on the ECM improvements?
<--- Score

62. How do you hand over ECM context?
<--- Score

63. Are task requirements clearly defined?
<--- Score

64. Has anyone else (internal or external to the organization) attempted to solve this problem or a similar one before? If so, what knowledge can be leveraged from these previous efforts?
<--- Score

65. How will the ECM team and the organization measure complete success of ECM?
<--- Score

66. Is data collected and displayed to better understand customer(s) critical needs and requirements.
<--- Score

67. Does workflow allow users to define conditions?
<--- Score

68. Have all basic functions of ECM been defined?
<--- Score

69. Why are you doing ECM and what is the scope?
<--- Score

70. How would you define the culture at your organization, how susceptible is it to ECM changes?
<--- Score

71. Are there different segments of customers?
<--- Score

72. How and when will the baselines be defined?
<--- Score

73. Is the team equipped with available and reliable resources?
<--- Score

74. What are the boundaries of the scope? What is in bounds and what is not? What is the start point? What is the stop point?
<--- Score

75. What are the Roles and Responsibilities for each team member and its leadership? Where is this documented?
<--- Score

76. Is ECM required?
<--- Score

77. Has a high-level 'as is' process map been completed, verified and validated?
<--- Score

78. What scope to assess?
<--- Score

79. Has the ECM work been fairly and/or equitably divided and delegated among team members who are qualified and capable to perform the work? Has everyone contributed?
<--- Score

80. Has a project plan, Gantt chart, or similar been developed/completed?
<--- Score

81. Are team charters developed?
<--- Score

82. When was the ECM start date?
<--- Score

83. What are the dynamics of the communication plan?
<--- Score

84. We have defined Capacity Management's Purpose, Goal and Objective
<--- Score

85. Are resources adequate for the scope?
<--- Score

86. When is the estimated completion date?
<--- Score

87. Are different versions of process maps needed to account for the different types of inputs?
<--- Score

88. What is the scope of the ECM effort?
<--- Score

89. How does the ECM manager ensure against scope creep?
<--- Score

90. Is there a ECM management charter, including

business case, problem and goal statements, scope, milestones, roles and responsibilities, communication plan?
<--- Score

91. Is there a completed, verified, and validated high-level 'as is' (not 'should be' or 'could be') business process map?
<--- Score

92. Are approval levels defined for contracts and supplements to contracts?
<--- Score

93. How do you think the partners involved in ECM would have defined success?
<--- Score

94. Have all of the relationships been defined properly?
<--- Score

95. What critical content must be communicated – who, what, when, where, and how?
<--- Score

96. Scope of sensitive information?
<--- Score

97. How do you keep key subject matter experts in the loop?
<--- Score

98. Is there a critical path to deliver ECM results?
<--- Score

99. Will team members regularly document their ECM work?
<--- Score

100. Is the team formed and are team leaders (Coaches and Management Leads) assigned?
<--- Score

101. How can the value of ECM be defined?
<--- Score

102. Is the current 'as is' process being followed? If not, what are the discrepancies?
<--- Score

103. What baselines are required to be defined and managed?
<--- Score

104. Is full participation by members in regularly held team meetings guaranteed?
<--- Score

105. Is there regularly 100% attendance at the team meetings? If not, have appointed substitutes attended to preserve cross-functionality and full representation?
<--- Score

106. What sources do you use to gather information for a ECM study?
<--- Score

107. What are the rough order estimates on cost savings/opportunities that ECM brings?
<--- Score

108. What would be the goal or target for a ECM's improvement team?
<--- Score

109. Is the scope of ECM defined?
<--- Score

110. What is the context?
<--- Score

111. Are accountability and ownership for ECM clearly defined?
<--- Score

112. We have defined Capacity Management's Scope
<--- Score

113. Are improvement team members fully trained on ECM?
<--- Score

114. Are customer(s) identified and segmented according to their different needs and requirements?
<--- Score

115. Are required metrics defined, what are they?
<--- Score

Add up total points for this section:
_ _ _ _ _ = Total points for this section

Divided by: _ _ _ _ _ _ (number of statements answered) = _ _ _ _ _ _
Average score for this section

Transfer your score to the ECM Index at
the beginning of the Self-Assessment.

CRITERION #3: MEASURE:

INTENT: Gather the correct data.
Measure the current performance and
evolution of the situation.

In my belief, the answer to this
question is clearly defined:

5 Strongly Agree

4 Agree

3 Neutral

2 Disagree

1 Strongly Disagree

1. What are the types and number of measures to use?
<--- Score

2. What causes extra work or rework?
<--- Score

3. Why do you expend time and effort to implement
measurement, for whom?
<--- Score

4. Is there a Performance Baseline?
<--- Score

5. How do you stay flexible and focused to recognize larger ECM results?
<--- Score

6. Where is it measured?
<--- Score

7. What harm might be caused?
<--- Score

8. How do you focus on what is right -not who is right?
<--- Score

9. Have the types of risks that may impact ECM been identified and analyzed?
<--- Score

10. How do you do risk analysis of rare, cascading, catastrophic events?
<--- Score

11. Who participated in the data collection for measurements?
<--- Score

12. What disadvantage does this cause for the user?
<--- Score

13. How do you measure progress and evaluate training effectiveness?
<--- Score

14. How to cause the change?
<--- Score

15. Are losses documented, analyzed, and remedial processes developed to prevent future losses?
<--- Score

16. What could cause delays in the schedule?
<--- Score

17. How is progress measured?
<--- Score

18. What charts has the team used to display the components of variation in the process?
<--- Score

19. Are missed ECM opportunities costing your organization money?
<--- Score

20. What would be a real cause for concern?
<--- Score

21. How will measures be used to manage and adapt?
<--- Score

22. How frequently do you track ECM measures?
<--- Score

23. Why do the measurements/indicators matter?
<--- Score

24. What are the key input variables? What are the key process variables? What are the key output variables?

<--- Score

25. Does ECM analysis isolate the fundamental causes of problems?
<--- Score

26. How large is the gap between current performance and the customer-specified (goal) performance?
<--- Score

27. Have you made assumptions about the shape of the future, particularly its impact on your customers and competitors?
<--- Score

28. How will success or failure be measured?
<--- Score

29. What key measures identified indicate the performance of the business process?
<--- Score

30. Does the ECM task fit the client's priorities?
<--- Score

31. How is the value delivered by ECM being measured?
<--- Score

32. Are key measures identified and agreed upon?
<--- Score

33. What has the team done to assure the stability and accuracy of the measurement process?
<--- Score

34. What could cause you to change course?
<--- Score

35. Are the units of measure consistent?
<--- Score

36. What causes investor action?
<--- Score

37. How will you measure success?
<--- Score

38. What perspective does your organization take to measure ECM success?
<--- Score

39. Have changes been properly/adequately analyzed for effect?
<--- Score

40. What measurements are possible, practicable and meaningful?
<--- Score

41. What are your key ECM organizational performance measures, including key short and longer-term financial measures?
<--- Score

42. Is Process Variation Displayed/Communicated?
<--- Score

43. How are measurements made?
<--- Score

44. Do you aggressively reward and promote the people who have the biggest impact on creating excellent ECM services/products?
<--- Score

45. Can you measure the return on analysis?
<--- Score

46. Can you do ECM without complex (expensive) analysis?
<--- Score

47. Have you found any 'ground fruit' or 'low-hanging fruit' for immediate remedies to the gap in performance?
<--- Score

48. Is data collection planned and executed?
<--- Score

49. Among the ECM product and service cost to be estimated, which is considered hardest to estimate?
<--- Score

50. What is an unallowable cost?
<--- Score

51. Are high impact defects defined and identified in the business process?
<--- Score

52. What is measured? Why?
<--- Score

53. What are the costs of reform?
<--- Score

54. Is it possible to estimate the impact of unanticipated complexity such as wrong or failed assumptions, feedback, etc. on proposed reforms?
<--- Score

55. What are the agreed upon definitions of the high impact areas, defect(s), unit(s), and opportunities that will figure into the process capability metrics?
<--- Score

56. Which stakeholder characteristics are analyzed?
<--- Score

57. Do you effectively measure and reward individual and team performance?
<--- Score

58. How can you measure the performance?
<--- Score

59. Who should receive measurement reports?
<--- Score

60. What do you measure and why?
<--- Score

61. Do staff have the necessary skills to collect, analyze, and report data?
<--- Score

62. What methods are feasible and acceptable to estimate the impact of reforms?
<--- Score

63. Are you taking your company in the direction of

better and revenue or cheaper and cost?
<--- Score

64. Are the measurements objective?
<--- Score

65. What are the uncertainties surrounding estimates of impact?
<--- Score

66. Is data collected on key measures that were identified?
<--- Score

67. What data was collected (past, present, future/ongoing)?
<--- Score

68. Did you tackle the cause or the symptom?
<--- Score

69. Was a data collection plan established?
<--- Score

70. How will effects be measured?
<--- Score

71. How do you identify and analyze stakeholders and their interests?
<--- Score

72. How will you measure your ECM effectiveness?
<--- Score

73. How do you measure lifecycle phases?
<--- Score

74. What are your key ECM indicators that you will measure, analyze and track?
<--- Score

75. While ECM can be a costly initiative, what are the costs of not properly managing your content?
<--- Score

76. The approach of traditional ECM works for detail complexity but is focused on a systematic approach rather than an understanding of the nature of systems themselves, what approach will permit your organization to deal with the kind of unpredictable emergent behaviors that dynamic complexity can introduce?
<--- Score

77. How can you measure ECM in a systematic way?
<--- Score

78. Is long term and short term variability accounted for?
<--- Score

79. How do you aggregate measures across priorities?
<--- Score

80. Are process variation components displayed/ communicated using suitable charts, graphs, plots?
<--- Score

81. How do you measure variability?
<--- Score

82. Which measures and indicators matter?

<--- Score

83. What evidence is there and what is measured?
<--- Score

84. How do you measure success?
<--- Score

85. How do your measurements capture actionable ECM information for use in exceeding your customers expectations and securing your customers engagement?
<--- Score

86. What are your customers expectations and measures?
<--- Score

87. Are you aware of what could cause a problem?
<--- Score

88. What measurements are being captured?
<--- Score

89. What causes mismanagement?
<--- Score

90. What particular quality tools did the team find helpful in establishing measurements?
<--- Score

91. Is the solution cost-effective?
<--- Score

92. How do you measure efficient delivery of ECM services?

<--- Score

93. Have the concerns of stakeholders to help identify and define potential barriers been obtained and analyzed?
<--- Score

94. Is key measure data collection planned and executed, process variation displayed and communicated and performance baselined?
<--- Score

95. What relevant entities could be measured?
<--- Score

96. Are there measurements based on task performance?
<--- Score

97. How do you control the overall costs of your work processes?
<--- Score

98. How will your organization measure success?
<--- Score

99. How is performance measured?
<--- Score

100. Is a solid data collection plan established that includes measurement systems analysis?
<--- Score

101. What is the right balance of time and resources between investigation, analysis, and discussion and dissemination?

<--- Score

102. How do you know that any ECM analysis is complete and comprehensive?
<--- Score

Add up total points for this section:
_____ = Total points for this section

Divided by: _____ (number of statements answered) = _____
Average score for this section

Transfer your score to the ECM Index at the beginning of the Self-Assessment.

CRITERION #4: ANALYZE:

INTENT: Analyze causes, assumptions and hypotheses.

In my belief, the answer to this question is clearly defined:

5 Strongly Agree

4 Agree

3 Neutral

2 Disagree

1 Strongly Disagree

1. What process should you select for improvement?
<--- Score

2. Did any additional data need to be collected?
<--- Score

3. Did any value-added analysis or 'lean thinking' take place to identify some of the gaps shown on the 'as is' process map?
<--- Score

4. How do you promote understanding that opportunity for improvement is not criticism of the status quo, or the people who created the status quo?
<--- Score

5. What are the revised rough estimates of the financial savings/opportunity for ECM improvements?
<--- Score

6. What were the crucial 'moments of truth' on the process map?
<--- Score

7. Is Data and process analysis, root cause analysis and quantifying the gap/opportunity in place?
<--- Score

8. What are the best opportunities for value improvement?
<--- Score

9. Think about some of the processes you undertake within your organization, which do you own?
<--- Score

10. Were Pareto charts (or similar) used to portray the 'heavy hitters' (or key sources of variation)?
<--- Score

11. Are you able to quickly capture all of your documents in your ECM system?
<--- Score

12. How do you implement and manage your work processes to ensure that they meet design

requirements?

<--- Score

13. What does the data say about the performance of the business process?

<--- Score

14. What ECM data do you gather or use now?

<--- Score

15. What meta-data is being created during backups and will be available when the documents are imported to the ECM system?

<--- Score

16. Do your leaders quickly bounce back from setbacks?

<--- Score

17. What controls do you have in place to protect data?

<--- Score

18. What are the primary business drivers of the organization in pursuing an ECMS?

<--- Score

19. Are gaps between current performance and the goal performance identified?

<--- Score

20. How is ECM data gathered?

<--- Score

21. Where is ECM data gathered?

<--- Score

22. What are your current levels and trends in key measures or indicators of ECM product and process performance that are important to and directly serve your customers? How do these results compare with the performance of your competitors and other organizations with similar offerings?
<--- Score

23. Is the gap/opportunity displayed and communicated in financial terms?
<--- Score

24. Have the problem and goal statements been updated to reflect the additional knowledge gained from the analyze phase?
<--- Score

25. Do several people in different organizational units assist with the ECM process?
<--- Score

26. How often will data be collected for measures?
<--- Score

27. Identify an operational issue in your organization. for example, could a particular task be done more quickly or more efficiently by ECM?
<--- Score

28. What successful thing are you doing today that may be blinding you to new growth opportunities?
<--- Score

29. Is the required ECM data gathered?
<--- Score

30. Do your employees have the opportunity to do what they do best everyday?
<--- Score

31. What other organizational variables, such as reward systems or communication systems, affect the performance of this ECM process?
<--- Score

32. What methods do you use to gather ECM data?
<--- Score

33. What quality tools were used to get through the analyze phase?
<--- Score

34. Is the performance gap determined?
<--- Score

35. Where is the data coming from to measure compliance?
<--- Score

36. Is the suppliers process defined and controlled?
<--- Score

37. What did the team gain from developing a sub-process map?
<--- Score

38. What is your organizations process which leads to recognition of value generation?
<--- Score

39. Can you add value to the current ECM decision-

making process (largely qualitative) by incorporating uncertainty modeling (more quantitative)?
<--- Score

40. A compounding model resolution with available relevant data can often provide insight towards a solution methodology; which ECM models, tools and techniques are necessary?
<--- Score

41. Do you, as a leader, bounce back quickly from setbacks?
<--- Score

42. What tools were used to generate the list of possible causes?
<--- Score

43. What data is gathered?
<--- Score

44. How do mission and objectives affect the ECM processes of your organization?
<--- Score

45. What are your key performance measures or indicators and in-process measures for the control and improvement of your ECM processes?
<--- Score

46. Is the ECM process severely broken such that a re-design is necessary?
<--- Score

47. Were there any improvement opportunities identified from the process analysis?

<--- Score

48. Was a detailed process map created to amplify critical steps of the 'as is' business process?
<--- Score

49. What were the financial benefits resulting from any 'ground fruit or low-hanging fruit' (quick fixes)?
<--- Score

50. Special attention needs to be paid to the inputs and outputs of each application that is, What content is necessary to support or drive the application?
<--- Score

51. Have any additional benefits been identified that will result from closing all or most of the gaps?
<--- Score

52. Do your contracts/agreements contain data security obligations?
<--- Score

53. How does the organization define, manage, and improve its ECM processes?
<--- Score

54. An organizationally feasible system request is one that considers the mission, goals and objectives of the organization. Key questions are: is the ECM solution request practical and will it solve a problem or take advantage of an opportunity to achieve company goals?
<--- Score

55. What tools were used to narrow the list of possible causes?
<--- Score

56. How was the detailed process map generated, verified, and validated?
<--- Score

57. What will drive ECM change?
<--- Score

58. What conclusions were drawn from the team's data collection and analysis? How did the team reach these conclusions?
<--- Score

59. What are your best practices for minimizing ECM project risk, while demonstrating incremental value and quick wins throughout the ECM project lifecycle?
<--- Score

60. How do your work systems and key work processes relate to and capitalize on your core competencies?
<--- Score

61. Record-keeping requirements flow from the records needed as inputs, outputs, controls and for transformation of a ECM process. Are the records needed as inputs to the ECM process available?
<--- Score

62. What are your ECM processes?
<--- Score

63. What other jobs or tasks affect the performance of

the steps in the ECM process?
<--- Score

64. Think about the functions involved in your ECM project, what processes flow from these functions?
<--- Score

65. Does the ECM support multiple naming and archiving processes?
<--- Score

66. How do you identify specific ECM investment opportunities and emerging trends?
<--- Score

67. Are ECM changes recognized early enough to be approved through the regular process?
<--- Score

68. What are your current levels and trends in key ECM measures or indicators of product and process performance that are important to and directly serve your customers?
<--- Score

69. Was a cause-and-effect diagram used to explore the different types of causes (or sources of variation)?
<--- Score

70. What is the cost of poor quality as supported by the team's analysis?
<--- Score

71. Were any designed experiments used to generate additional insight into the data analysis?
<--- Score

Add up total points for this section:
_____ = Total points for this section

Divided by: _____ (number of
statements answered) = _____
Average score for this section

Transfer your score to the ECM Index at
the beginning of the Self-Assessment.

CRITERION #5: IMPROVE:

INTENT: Develop a practical solution.
Innovate, establish and test the
solution and to measure the results.

In my belief, the answer to this
question is clearly defined:

5 Strongly Agree

4 Agree

3 Neutral

2 Disagree

1 Strongly Disagree

1. Which of the recognised risks out of all risks can be most likely transferred?
<--- Score

2. How will you know that you have improved?
<--- Score

3. Are new and improved process ('should be') maps developed?

<--- Score

4. What error proofing will be done to address some of the discrepancies observed in the 'as is' process?
<--- Score

5. What communications are necessary to support the implementation of the solution?
<--- Score

6. How do you link measurement and risk?
<--- Score

7. Who controls key decisions that will be made?
<--- Score

8. How do you improve your likelihood of success ?
<--- Score

9. What are the implications of the one critical ECM decision 10 minutes, 10 months, and 10 years from now?
<--- Score

10. What actually has to improve and by how much?
<--- Score

11. How can skill-level changes improve ECM?
<--- Score

12. Are the best solutions selected?
<--- Score

13. What tools were most useful during the improve phase?
<--- Score

14. Do those selected for the ECM team have a good general understanding of what ECM is all about?
<--- Score

15. How do you keep improving ECM?
<--- Score

16. What is the annual research & development (R&D) investment for the solution being used, both in terms of financial investment and total number of employees dedicated to the R&D function?
<--- Score

17. What were the underlying assumptions on the cost-benefit analysis?
<--- Score

18. What went well, what should change, what can improve?
<--- Score

19. What is the team's contingency plan for potential problems occurring in implementation?
<--- Score

20. What tools were used to evaluate the potential solutions?
<--- Score

21. Is a contingency plan established?
<--- Score

22. What are your current levels and trends in key measures or indicators of workforce and leader development?

<--- Score

23. Does the goal represent a desired result that can be measured?
<--- Score

24. Can you identify any significant risks or exposures to ECM third- parties (vendors, service providers, alliance partners etc) that concern you?
<--- Score

25. Who will be responsible for documenting the ECM requirements in detail?
<--- Score

26. Does the ECM provide imaging software to import basic scanned documents?
<--- Score

27. Was a pilot designed for the proposed solution(s)?
<--- Score

28. How will the organization know that the solution worked?
<--- Score

29. What do you want to improve?
<--- Score

30. Can the solution be designed and implemented within an acceptable time period?
<--- Score

31. What is the magnitude of the improvements?
<--- Score

32. How do you measure risk?
<--- Score

33. How do the ECM results compare with the performance of your competitors and other organizations with similar offerings?
<--- Score

34. Are you assessing ECM and risk?
<--- Score

35. What tools were used to tap into the creativity and encourage 'outside the box' thinking?
<--- Score

36. Is a solution implementation plan established, including schedule/work breakdown structure, resources, risk management plan, cost/budget, and control plan?
<--- Score

37. Where are mission-critical documents when you need them?
<--- Score

38. How does document automation manage integration with other line-of-business applications in an organization (e.g., ERP, CRM)?
<--- Score

39. How does the solution manage documents with a retention policy?
<--- Score

40. How will you know when its improved?
<--- Score

41. Are risk triggers captured?
<--- Score

42. What is the risk?
<--- Score

43. How will the team or the process owner(s) monitor the implementation plan to see that it is working as intended?
<--- Score

44. How do you manage and improve your ECM work systems to deliver customer value and achieve organizational success and sustainability?
<--- Score

45. Who will be responsible for making the decisions to include or exclude requested changes once ECM is underway?
<--- Score

46. Will the controls trigger any other risks?
<--- Score

47. Is the implementation plan designed?
<--- Score

48. Is the optimal solution selected based on testing and analysis?
<--- Score

49. How can you improve ECM?
<--- Score

50. What lessons, if any, from a pilot were

incorporated into the design of the full-scale solution?
<--- Score

51. What can you do to improve?
<--- Score

52. How do you improve productivity?
<--- Score

53. How did the team generate the list of possible solutions?
<--- Score

54. Does the ECM allow access to documents via a web browser?
<--- Score

55. How do you define the solutions' scope?
<--- Score

56. Is the scope clearly documented?
<--- Score

57. How do you go about comparing ECM approaches/solutions?
<--- Score

58. What improvements have been achieved?
<--- Score

59. Why improve in the first place?
<--- Score

60. Is pilot data collected and analyzed?
<--- Score

61. Does the ECM allow access to documents via web browser?

<--- Score

62. Who controls the risk?
<--- Score

63. Describe the design of the pilot and what tests were conducted, if any?
<--- Score

64. Does your document automation support public-facing E-forms that can be filled out and submitted on line?

<--- Score

65. What is the ECM's sustainability risk?
<--- Score

66. What attendant changes will need to be made to ensure that the solution is successful?
<--- Score

67. Are improved process ('should be') maps modified based on pilot data and analysis?
<--- Score

68. Which piece (or pieces) of the ECM technology pie does your solution address?

<--- Score

69. Does the ECM allow access to documents by an Apple iOS or Android device?

<--- Score

70. What is the implementation plan?

<--- Score

71. Do any of the backfile converted documents contain annotations that must be transferred to the ECM system?
<--- Score

72. How do you measure improved ECM service perception, and satisfaction?
<--- Score

73. Is the measure of success for ECM understandable to a variety of people?
<--- Score

74. Is the solution technically practical?
<--- Score

75. How do you improve ECM service perception, and satisfaction?
<--- Score

76. Is there a small-scale pilot for proposed improvement(s)? What conclusions were drawn from the outcomes of a pilot?
<--- Score

77. Risk Identification: What are the possible risk events your organization faces in relation to ECM?
<--- Score

78. Risk events: what are the things that could go wrong?
<--- Score

79. How will you know that a change is an

improvement?
<--- Score

80. Is there a cost/benefit analysis of optimal solution(s)?
<--- Score

81. Does your ECMS support document-centric, author-review and approve automated workflow capabilities?
<--- Score

82. If you could go back in time five years, what decision would you make differently? What is your best guess as to what decision you're making today you might regret five years from now?
<--- Score

83. To what extent does management recognize ECM as a tool to increase the results?
<--- Score

84. Is supporting ECM documentation required?
<--- Score

85. How significant is the improvement in the eyes of the end user?
<--- Score

86. What needs improvement? Why?
<--- Score

87. What practices helps your organization to develop its capacity to recognize patterns?
<--- Score

88. How do you know which Document Automation solution(s) is/are best for our size of business?
<--- Score

89. In the past few months, what is the smallest change you have made that has had the biggest positive result? What was it about that small change that produced the large return?
<--- Score

90. What resources are required for the improvement efforts?
<--- Score

91. Were any criteria developed to assist the team in testing and evaluating potential solutions?
<--- Score

92. Are possible solutions generated and tested?
<--- Score

93. How does the team improve its work?
<--- Score

94. How can you improve performance?
<--- Score

95. Who will be using the results of the measurement activities?
<--- Score

96. For decision problems, how do you develop a decision statement?
<--- Score

97. What is ECM's impact on utilizing the best solution(s)?
<--- Score

98. Is there a high likelihood that any recommendations will achieve their intended results?
<--- Score

99. How does the solution remove the key sources of issues discovered in the analyze phase?
<--- Score

100. What does the 'should be' process map/design look like?
<--- Score

101. Can workflow be automated for a specific document type and workflow template?
<--- Score

102. Are there any constraints (technical, political, cultural, or otherwise) that would inhibit certain solutions?
<--- Score

103. Who are the people involved in developing and implementing ECM?
<--- Score

104. For estimation problems, how do you develop an estimation statement?
<--- Score

105. How will you measure the results?
<--- Score

Add up total points for this section:
_____ = Total points for this section

Divided by: _____ (number of statements answered) = _____
Average score for this section

Transfer your score to the ECM Index at the beginning of the Self-Assessment.

CRITERION #6: CONTROL:

INTENT: Implement the practical solution. Maintain the performance and correct possible complications.

In my belief, the answer to this question is clearly defined:

5 Strongly Agree

4 Agree

3 Neutral

2 Disagree

1 Strongly Disagree

1. Has the system been through SA&A (Security Assessment and Authorization) or ECM-R (Enterprise Continuous Monitoring Reauthorization)?
<--- Score

2. What adjustments to the strategies are needed?
<--- Score

3. Does ECM appropriately measure and monitor risk?
<--- Score

4. Is there a transfer of ownership and knowledge to process owner and process team tasked with the responsibilities.
<--- Score

5. Are documented procedures clear and easy to follow for the operators?
<--- Score

6. How do senior leaders actions reflect a commitment to the organizations ECM values?
<--- Score

7. Does the ECM performance meet the customer's requirements?
<--- Score

8. Who controls critical resources?
<--- Score

9. How will report readings be checked to effectively monitor performance?
<--- Score

10. Is reporting being used or needed?
<--- Score

11. Are pertinent alerts monitored, analyzed and distributed to appropriate personnel?
<--- Score

12. Can you adapt and adjust to changing ECM situations?

<--- Score

13. What key inputs and outputs are being measured on an ongoing basis?
<--- Score

14. Does job training on the documented procedures need to be part of the process team's education and training?
<--- Score

15. How do controls support value?
<--- Score

16. Are the planned controls in place?
<--- Score

17. Do you monitor the ECM decisions made and fine tune them as they evolve?
<--- Score

18. You may have created your quality measures at a time when you lacked resources, technology wasn't up to the required standard, or low service levels were the industry norm. Have those circumstances changed?
<--- Score

19. How do you establish and deploy modified action plans if circumstances require a shift in plans and rapid execution of new plans?
<--- Score

20. How will input, process, and output variables be checked to detect for sub-optimal conditions?
<--- Score

21. What is the best design framework for ECM organization now that, in a post industrial-age if the top-down, command and control model is no longer relevant?
<--- Score

22. What should you measure to verify efficiency gains?
<--- Score

23. Is there a standardized process?
<--- Score

24. How will the process owner and team be able to hold the gains?
<--- Score

25. Is a response plan established and deployed?
<--- Score

26. Do you monitor the effectiveness of your ECM activities?
<--- Score

27. What are the critical parameters to watch?
<--- Score

28. What is the control/monitoring plan?
<--- Score

29. What quality tools were useful in the control phase?
<--- Score

30. Will the team be available to assist members in

planning investigations?
<--- Score

31. Where do ideas that reach policy makers and planners as proposals for ECM strengthening and reform actually originate?
<--- Score

32. Is there a ECM Communication plan covering who needs to get what information when?
<--- Score

33. What do your reports reflect?
<--- Score

34. Are new process steps, standards, and documentation ingrained into normal operations?
<--- Score

35. What can you control?
<--- Score

36. Is there a documented and implemented monitoring plan?
<--- Score

37. How likely is the current ECM plan to come in on schedule or on budget?
<--- Score

38. Can support from partners be adjusted?
<--- Score

39. Have new or revised work instructions resulted?
<--- Score

40. How do your controls stack up?
<--- Score

41. Is there a recommended audit plan for routine surveillance inspections of ECM's gains?
<--- Score

42. What should the next improvement project be that is related to ECM?
<--- Score

43. Will any special training be provided for results interpretation?
<--- Score

44. How do you select, collect, align, and integrate ECM data and information for tracking daily operations and overall organizational performance, including progress relative to strategic objectives and action plans?
<--- Score

45. What is the recommended frequency of auditing?
<--- Score

46. Do the ECM decisions you make today help people and the planet tomorrow?
<--- Score

47. What do you stand for--and what are you against?
<--- Score

48. Who sets the ECM standards?
<--- Score

49. How will you measure your QA plan's

effectiveness?

<--- Score

50. In the case of a ECM project, the criteria for the audit derive from implementation objectives. an audit of a ECM project involves assessing whether the recommendations outlined for implementation have been met. Can you track that any ECM project is implemented as planned, and is it working?

<--- Score

51. Is a response plan in place for when the input, process, or output measures indicate an 'out-of-control' condition?

<--- Score

52. Are operating procedures consistent?

<--- Score

53. Implementation Planning: is a pilot needed to test the changes before a full roll out occurs?

<--- Score

54. Who will be in control?

<--- Score

55. Does the response plan contain a definite closed loop continual improvement scheme (e.g., plan-do-check-act)?

<--- Score

56. Has the improved process and its steps been standardized?

<--- Score

57. Who has control over resources?

<--- Score

58. What do you measure to verify effectiveness gains?
<--- Score

59. How might the organization capture best practices and lessons learned so as to leverage improvements across the business?
<--- Score

60. Is new knowledge gained imbedded in the response plan?
<--- Score

61. Does a troubleshooting guide exist or is it needed?
<--- Score

62. Who is the ECM process owner?
<--- Score

63. What are you attempting to measure/monitor?
<--- Score

64. What other areas of the organization might benefit from the ECM team's improvements, knowledge, and learning?
<--- Score

65. What is your theory of human motivation, and how does your compensation plan fit with that view?
<--- Score

66. Is there a control plan in place for sustaining improvements (short and long-term)?
<--- Score

67. Is there documentation that will support the successful operation of the improvement?
<--- Score

68. Are the planned controls working?
<--- Score

69. Is knowledge gained on process shared and institutionalized?
<--- Score

70. How do you plan on providing proper recognition and disclosure of supporting companies?
<--- Score

71. Will your goals reflect your program budget?
<--- Score

72. How will the day-to-day responsibilities for monitoring and continual improvement be transferred from the improvement team to the process owner?
<--- Score

73. Are there documented procedures?
<--- Score

74. What other systems, operations, processes, and infrastructures (hiring practices, staffing, training, incentives/rewards, metrics/dashboards/scorecards, etc.) need updates, additions, changes, or deletions in order to facilitate knowledge transfer and improvements?
<--- Score

75. How is change control managed?
<--- Score

76. Does the system allow users to perform workflow activities using a standard web browser such as Internet Explorer and Mozilla Firefox?
<--- Score

77. Act/Adjust: What Do you Need to Do Differently?
<--- Score

78. How will new or emerging customer needs/ requirements be checked/communicated to orient the process toward meeting the new specifications and continually reducing variation?
<--- Score

79. How will the process owner verify improvement in present and future sigma levels, process capabilities?
<--- Score

80. Are suggested corrective/restorative actions indicated on the response plan for known causes to problems that might surface?
<--- Score

81. Are controls in place and consistently applied?
<--- Score

Add up total points for this section:
_ _ _ _ _ = Total points for this section

Divided by: _ _ _ _ _ _ (number of statements answered) = _ _ _ _ _ _
Average score for this section

Transfer your score to the ECM Index at
the beginning of the Self-Assessment.

CRITERION #7: SUSTAIN:

INTENT: Retain the benefits.

In my belief, the answer to this question is clearly defined:

5 Strongly Agree

4 Agree

3 Neutral

2 Disagree

1 Strongly Disagree

1. How important is ECM to the user organizations mission?
<--- Score

2. What scanners does your organization currently have in use that will be integrated with the ECM system?
<--- Score

3. What was the last experiment you ran?
<--- Score

4. Who, on the executive team or the board, has spoken to a customer recently?
<--- Score

5. Political -is anyone trying to undermine this project?
<--- Score

6. What is effective ECM?
<--- Score

7. At what moment would you think; Will I get fired?
<--- Score

8. What are the essentials of internal ECM management?
<--- Score

9. In the past year, what have you done (or could you have done) to increase the accurate perception of your company/brand as ethical and honest?
<--- Score

10. What should you stop doing?
<--- Score

11. Can you break it down?
<--- Score

12. How will you motivate the stakeholders with the least vested interest?
<--- Score

13. Who uses your product in ways you never expected?

<--- Score

14. Are assumptions made in ECM stated explicitly?
<--- Score

15. Has implementation been effective in reaching specified objectives so far?
<--- Score

16. What trouble can you get into?
<--- Score

17. What would you recommend your friend do if he/she were facing this dilemma?
<--- Score

18. If you weren't already in this business, would you enter it today? And if not, what are you going to do about it?
<--- Score

19. How do you foster the skills, knowledge, talents, attributes, and characteristics you want to have?
<--- Score

20. What are the potential basics of ECM fraud?
<--- Score

21. Who do you think the world wants your organization to be?
<--- Score

22. What is it like to work for you?
<--- Score

23. Instead of going to current contacts for new ideas,

what if you reconnected with dormant contacts--
the people you used to know? If you were going
reactivate a dormant tie, who would it be?
<--- Score

24. Whom among your colleagues do you trust, and
for what?
<--- Score

25. What are your personal philosophies regarding
ECM and how do they influence your work?
<--- Score

26. Do you have the right people on the bus?
<--- Score

27. What is the range of capabilities?
<--- Score

28. How do you make it meaningful in connecting
ECM with what users do day-to-day?
<--- Score

29. How do you lead with ECM in mind?
<--- Score

30. Are you paying enough attention to the partners
your company depends on to succeed?
<--- Score

31. Ask yourself: how would you do this work if you
only had one staff member to do it?
<--- Score

32. What new services of functionality will be
implemented next with ECM ?

<--- Score

33. How do you listen to customers to obtain actionable information?
<--- Score

34. Who is responsible for errors?
<--- Score

35. How will you know that the ECM project has been successful?
<--- Score

36. How do you deal with ECM changes?
<--- Score

37. Which functions and people interact with the supplier and or customer?
<--- Score

38. What are internal and external ECM relations?
<--- Score

39. What is the craziest thing you can do?
<--- Score

40. What Are the Benefits of Using AECMA Simplified English?
<--- Score

41. How do you cross-sell and up-sell your ECM success?
<--- Score

42. Is your basic point _____ or _____?
<--- Score

43. What do we do when new problems arise?
<--- Score

44. If you had to leave your organization for a year and the only communication you could have with employees/colleagues was a single paragraph, what would you write?
<--- Score

45. Who will provide the final approval of ECM deliverables?
<--- Score

46. Are you making progress, and are you making progress as ECM leaders?
<--- Score

47. Does the ECM accommodate Full Text Indexing (i.e. OCR) to search for and retrieve files?
<--- Score

48. Are you changing as fast as the world around you?
<--- Score

49. Have benefits been optimized with all key stakeholders?
<--- Score

50. What must you excel at?
<--- Score

51. Are your responses positive or negative?
<--- Score

52. How do you govern and fulfill your societal

responsibilities?
<--- Score

53. In what application areas do want to use an ECMS?
<--- Score

54. Were lessons learned captured and communicated?
<--- Score

55. What are the success criteria that will indicate that ECM objectives have been met and the benefits delivered?
<--- Score

56. Is a ECM team work effort in place?
<--- Score

57. Are the assumptions believable and achievable?
<--- Score

58. Does the system have the capability to do batch scanning and indexing?
<--- Score

59. What have been your experiences in defining long range ECM goals?
<--- Score

60. How do you address records management?
<--- Score

61. How do you track customer value, profitability or financial return, organizational success, and sustainability?

<--- Score

62. If you got fired and a new hire took your place, what would she do different?
<--- Score

63. What happens when a new employee joins the organization?
<--- Score

64. What ECM modifications can you make work for you?
<--- Score

65. How do you create buy-in?
<--- Score

66. Are there any disadvantages to implementing ECM? There might be some that are less obvious?
<--- Score

67. To whom do you add value?
<--- Score

68. What are you trying to prove to yourself, and how might it be hijacking your life and business success?
<--- Score

69. How do you stay inspired?
<--- Score

70. What relationships among ECM trends do you perceive?
<--- Score

71. What are the top 3 things at the forefront of your

ECM agendas for the next 3 years?
<--- Score

72. Do you have enough freaky customers in your portfolio pushing you to the limit day in and day out?
<--- Score

73. Would you rather sell to knowledgeable and informed customers or to uninformed customers?
<--- Score

74. How does ECM integrate with other business initiatives?
<--- Score

75. Does syntactic rewriting affect English for science and technology text comprehension?
<--- Score

76. Will the system accommodate full text OCR to search for and retrieve files?
<--- Score

77. Do you feel that more should be done in the ECM area?
<--- Score

78. What happens at your organization when people fail?
<--- Score

79. What are the usability implications of ECM actions?
<--- Score

80. What projects are going on in the organization today, and what resources are those projects using

from the resource pools?
<--- Score

81. How will you ensure you get what you expected?
<--- Score

82. Why do and why don't your customers like your organization?
<--- Score

83. What are the challenges?
<--- Score

84. What unique value proposition (UVP) do you offer?
<--- Score

85. How can you become more high-tech but still be high touch?
<--- Score

86. Are the criteria for selecting recommendations stated?
<--- Score

87. What are the key enablers to make this ECM move?
<--- Score

88. What does your signature ensure?
<--- Score

89. What are the short and long-term ECM goals?
<--- Score

90. Why is it important to have senior management support for a ECM project?
<--- Score

91. How do you keep records, of what?
<--- Score

92. What stupid rule would you most like to kill?
<--- Score

93. How many employees do you have assigned to your ECM suite related tasks and what are their roles?
<--- Score

94. What ECM skills are most important?
<--- Score

95. Who is responsible for ensuring appropriate resources (time, people and money) are allocated to ECM?
<--- Score

96. How do you transition from the baseline to the target?
<--- Score

97. What is the difference between an enterprise content management system ecms and a content management system cms?
<--- Score

98. What is AECMA Simplified English?
<--- Score

99. What are current ECM paradigms?
<--- Score

100. Is maximizing ECM protection the same as

minimizing ECM loss?
<--- Score

101. How can you best use all of your knowledge repositories to enhance learning and sharing?
<--- Score

102. Who will manage the integration of tools?
<--- Score

103. Have new benefits been realized?
<--- Score

104. How can you become the company that would put you out of business?
<--- Score

105. What are strategies for increasing support and reducing opposition?
<--- Score

106. Whose voice (department, ethnic group, women, older workers, etc) might you have missed hearing from in your company, and how might you amplify this voice to create positive momentum for your business?
<--- Score

107. Do ECM rules make a reasonable demand on a users capabilities?
<--- Score

108. What role does communication play in the success or failure of a ECM project?
<--- Score

109. Who is responsible for ECM?
<--- Score

110. Who are your customers?
<--- Score

111. How do you set ECM stretch targets and how do you get people to not only participate in setting these stretch targets but also that they strive to achieve these?
<--- Score

112. How do you decide how much to remunerate an employee?
<--- Score

113. Where can you break convention?
<--- Score

114. Which individuals, teams or departments will be involved in ECM?
<--- Score

115. Do your E-forms support E-signatures?
<--- Score

116. Are you satisfied with your current role? If not, what is missing from it?
<--- Score

117. What you are going to do to affect the numbers?
<--- Score

118. Do you have the right capabilities and capacities?
<--- Score

119. How likely is it that a customer would recommend your company to a friend or colleague?
<--- Score

120. Think of your ECM project, what are the main functions?
<--- Score

121. Will it be accepted by users?
<--- Score

122. Is there any reason to believe the opposite of my current belief?
<--- Score

123. How will you insure seamless interoperability of ECM moving forward?
<--- Score

124. What type of ECMS do you think is best for your organization?
<--- Score

125. How do customers see your organization?
<--- Score

126. Is ECM dependent on the successful delivery of a current project?
<--- Score

127. Do you think ECM accomplishes the goals you expect it to accomplish?
<--- Score

128. How is implementation research currently incorporated into each of your goals?

<--- Score

129. What is something you believe that nearly no one agrees with you on?
<--- Score

130. If you were responsible for initiating and implementing major changes in your organization, what steps might you take to ensure acceptance of those changes?
<--- Score

131. Why is ECM important for you now?
<--- Score

132. Can you do all this work?
<--- Score

133. Do you have past ECM successes?
<--- Score

134. What trophy do you want on your mantle?
<--- Score

135. Does the system provide the ability to capture index information from scanning/capture software?
<--- Score

136. Who are the key stakeholders?
<--- Score

137. Does it give your organization a distinct competitive edge that comes from working faster and more efficiently than your competition?
<--- Score

138. How do you know if you are successful?
<--- Score

139. How do you go about securing ECM?
<--- Score

140. Does the ECM allow users to configure custom searches that they commonly use?
<--- Score

141. Does the ECM offer web-based and desktop client interface search and retrieval?
<--- Score

142. What goals did you miss?
<--- Score

143. What are your most important goals for the strategic ECM objectives?
<--- Score

144. What are the long-term ECM goals?
<--- Score

145. Do you say no to customers for no reason?
<--- Score

146. If no one would ever find out about your accomplishments, how would you lead differently?
<--- Score

147. Which models, tools and techniques are necessary?
<--- Score

148. If your company went out of business tomorrow, would anyone who doesn't get a paycheck here care?
<--- Score

149. Can the schedule be done in the given time?
<--- Score

150. Are you maintaining a past–present–future perspective throughout the ECM discussion?
<--- Score

151. Who will determine interim and final deadlines?
<--- Score

152. What are the rules and assumptions your industry operates under? What if the opposite were true?
<--- Score

153. Who do we want your customers to become?
<--- Score

154. What are the business goals ECM is aiming to achieve?
<--- Score

155. How do you proactively clarify deliverables and ECM quality expectations?
<--- Score

156. What is the estimated value of the project?
<--- Score

157. What is your question? Why?
<--- Score

158. Do you think you know, or do you know you

know ?
<--- Score

159. How long will it take to change?
<--- Score

160. What will be the consequences to the stakeholder (financial, reputation etc) if ECM does not go ahead or fails to deliver the objectives?
<--- Score

161. If there were zero limitations, what would you do differently?
<--- Score

162. Is there a work around that you can use?
<--- Score

163. How much does ECM help?
<--- Score

164. If you do not follow, then how to lead?
<--- Score

165. What is an unauthorized commitment?
<--- Score

166. What threat is ECM addressing?
<--- Score

167. What is the recommended frequency of auditing?
<--- Score

168. Who have you, as a company, historically been when you've been at your best?
<--- Score

169. Is the ECM organization completing tasks effectively and efficiently?

<--- Score

170. In retrospect, of the projects that you pulled the plug on, what percent do you wish had been allowed to keep going, and what percent do you wish had ended earlier?

<--- Score

171. What kind of crime could a potential new hire have committed that would not only not disqualify him/her from being hired by your organization, but would actually indicate that he/she might be a particularly good fit?

<--- Score

172. What are you challenging?

<--- Score

173. How does your organization ensure user acceptance?

<--- Score

174. How do you engage the workforce, in addition to satisfying them?

<--- Score

175. What models of scanners does you currently have in use that will be integrated with the new system?

<--- Score

176. What are the barriers to increased ECM production?

<--- Score

177. Are you / should you be revolutionary or evolutionary?
<--- Score

178. What happens if you do not have enough funding?
<--- Score

179. How can you incorporate support to ensure safe and effective use of ECM into the services that you provide?
<--- Score

180. What is the source of the strategies for ECM strengthening and reform?
<--- Score

181. Who do you want your customers to become?
<--- Score

182. Who will be responsible for deciding whether ECM goes ahead or not after the initial investigations?
<--- Score

183. How do you assess the ECM pitfalls that are inherent in implementing it?
<--- Score

184. Do you know what you are doing? And who do you call if you don't?
<--- Score

185. Marketing budgets are tighter, consumers are more skeptical, and social media has changed

forever the way we talk about ECM. How do you gain traction?

<--- Score

186. Does the ECM fully integrate with Microsoft Exchange?

<--- Score

187. What are specific ECM rules to follow?

<--- Score

188. Are you relevant? Will you be relevant five years from now? Ten?

<--- Score

189. What current systems have to be understood and/or changed?

<--- Score

190. Did your employees make progress today?

<--- Score

191. Are there any activities that you can take off your to do list?

<--- Score

192. Do you see more potential in people than they do in themselves?

<--- Score

193. How much contingency will be available in the budget?

<--- Score

194. Have your thoughts on where to use an ECMS changed?

<--- Score

195. Are all key stakeholders present at all Structured Walkthroughs?
<--- Score

196. What counts that you are not counting?
<--- Score

197. What one word do you want to own in the minds of your customers, employees, and partners?
<--- Score

198. Is it economical; do you have the time and money?
<--- Score

199. What would have to be true for the option on the table to be the best possible choice?
<--- Score

200. What management system can you use to leverage the ECM experience, ideas, and concerns of the people closest to the work to be done?
<--- Score

201. What have you done to protect your business from competitive encroachment?
<--- Score

202. What is a feasible sequencing of reform initiatives over time?
<--- Score

203. What information is critical to your organization that your executives are ignoring?

<--- Score

204. Will there be any necessary staff changes (redundancies or new hires)?
<--- Score

205. How do you accomplish your long range ECM goals?
<--- Score

206. Where necessary or desirable can search capability be tailored to limit the areas of the ECM which are searched?
<--- Score

207. Why should people listen to you?
<--- Score

208. How do you ensure that implementations of ECM products are done in a way that ensures safety?
<--- Score

209. Why will customers want to buy your organizations products/services?
<--- Score

210. How many employees do you have assigned to your ECM Suite related tasks?
<--- Score

211. Who else should you help?
<--- Score

212. How do you provide a safe environment -physically and emotionally?
<--- Score

213. Who is on the team?
<--- Score

214. Which ECM goals are the most important?
<--- Score

215. What are the gaps in your knowledge and experience?
<--- Score

216. Why not do ECM?
<--- Score

217. How do you keep the momentum going?
<--- Score

218. Who are four people whose careers you have enhanced?
<--- Score

219. If your customer were your grandmother, would you tell her to buy what you're selling?
<--- Score

220. What is the purpose of ECM in relation to the mission?
<--- Score

221. What business benefits will ECM goals deliver if achieved?
<--- Score

222. How are you doing compared to your industry?
<--- Score

223. How can you negotiate ECM successfully with a stubborn boss, an irate client, or a deceitful coworker?
<--- Score

224. What is the funding source for this project?
<--- Score

225. Are new benefits received and understood?
<--- Score

226. What is the kind of project structure that would be appropriate for your ECM project, should it be formal and complex, or can it be less formal and relatively simple?
<--- Score

227. Is ECM realistic, or are you setting yourself up for failure?
<--- Score

228. Does the ECM fully integrate with Microsoft Office applications (Word, Excel, PowerPoint, etc.)?
<--- Score

229. What did you miss in the interview for the worst hire you ever made?
<--- Score

230. What is your competitive advantage?
<--- Score

231. When information truly is ubiquitous, when reach and connectivity are completely global, when computing resources are infinite, and when a whole new set of impossibilities are not only possible, but happening, what will that do to your business?

<--- Score

232. Why should you adopt a ECM framework?
<--- Score

233. What is your formula for success in ECM ?
<--- Score

234. How do you determine the key elements that affect ECM workforce satisfaction, how are these elements determined for different workforce groups and segments?
<--- Score

235. Operational - will it work?
<--- Score

236. When you map the key players in your own work and the types/domains of relationships with them, which relationships do you find easy and which challenging, and why?
<--- Score

237. Is the impact that ECM has shown?
<--- Score

238. Does the workflow include E-signature capabilities?
<--- Score

Add up total points for this section:
_ _ _ _ _ = Total points for this section

Divided by: _ _ _ _ _ _ (number of statements answered) = _ _ _ _ _ _
Average score for this section

Transfer your score to the ECM Index at
the beginning of the Self-Assessment.

ECM and Managing Projects, Criteria for Project Managers:

1.0 Initiating Process Group: ECM

1. How will it affect me?

2. Contingency planning. if a risk event occurs, what will you do?

3. What are the short and long term implications?

4. What were the challenges that you encountered during the execution of a previous ECM project that you would not want to repeat?

5. Mitigate. what will you do to minimize the impact should the risk event occur?

6. Are you certain deliverables are properly completed and meet quality standards?

7. What were things that you need to improve?

8. Were sponsors and decision makers available when needed outside regularly scheduled meetings?

9. If the risk event occurs, what will you do?

10. What is the NEXT thing to do?

11. What were things that you did very well and want to do the same again on the next ECM project?

12. Are identified risks being monitored properly, are new risks arising during the ECM project or are foreseen risks occurring?

13. Are there resources to maintain and support the outcome of the ECM project?

14. Who is involved in each phase?

15. What will be the pressing issues of tomorrow?

16. Are stakeholders properly informed about the status of the ECM project?

17. What input will you be required to provide the ECM project team?

18. Were decisions made in a timely manner?

19. In which ECM project management process group is the detailed ECM project budget created?

20. Realistic - are the desired results expressed in a way that the team will be motivated and believe that the required level of involvement will be obtained?

1.1 Project Charter: ECM

21. What are you striving to accomplish (measurable goal(s))?

22. Are you building in-house ?

23. Customer benefits: what customer requirements does this ECM project address?

24. What date will the task finish?

25. Did your ECM project ask for this?

26. What metrics could you look at?

27. Who is the sponsor?

28. Are there special technology requirements?

29. Strategic fit: what is the strategic initiative identifier for this ECM project?

30. How do you manage integration?

31. Assumptions: what factors, for planning purposes, are you considering to be true?

32. How will you know a change is an improvement?

33. How much?

34. Must Have?

35. Is it an improvement over existing products?

36. Why use a ECM project charter?

37. ECM project deliverables: what is the ECM project going to produce?

38. Environmental stewardship and sustainability considerations: what is the process that will be used to ensure compliance with the environmental stewardship policy?

39. Will this replace an existing product?

40. What are the known stakeholder requirements?

1.2 Stakeholder Register: ECM

41. Is your organization ready for change?

42. Who is managing stakeholder engagement?

43. Who wants to talk about Security?

44. What are the major ECM project milestones requiring communications or providing communications opportunities?

45. How big is the gap?

46. How will reports be created?

47. What is the power of the stakeholder?

48. What & Why?

49. How should employers make voices heard?

50. What opportunities exist to provide communications?

51. Who are the stakeholders?

52. How much influence do they have on the ECM project?

1.3 Stakeholder Analysis Matrix: ECM

53. Disadvantages of proposition?

54. Timescales, deadlines and pressures?

55. What is accountability in relation to the ECM project?

56. Do recommendations include actions to address any differential distribution of impacts?

57. Does the stakeholder want to be involved or merely need to be informed about the ECM project and its process?

58. Arena: in what fields are the actors active, where are they present?

59. Experience, knowledge, data?

60. Are there different rules or organizational models for men and women?

61. What obstacles does your organization face?

62. Cultural, attitudinal, behavioural?

63. How to measure the achievement of the Outputs?

64. Identify the stakeholders levels most frequently used –or at least sought– in your ECM projects and for which purpose?

65. Are there people who ise voices or interests in the issue may not be heard?

66. Which conditions out of the control of the management are crucial to contribute for the achievement of the development objective?

67. What makes a person a stakeholder?

68. Philosophy and values?

69. Are they likely to influence the success or failure of your ECM project?

70. How to measure the achievement of the Immediate Objective?

71. Reputation, presence and reach?

72. Do the stakeholders goals and expectations support or conflict with the ECM project goals?

2.0 Planning Process Group: ECM

73. To what extent do the intervention objectives and strategies of the ECM project respond to your organizations plans?

74. How many days can task X be late in starting without affecting the ECM project completion date?

75. Are the necessary foundations in place to ensure the sustainability of the results of the ECM project?

76. Are you just doing busywork to pass the time?

77. What is the critical path for this ECM project, and what is the duration of the critical path?

78. What makes your ECM project successful?

79. What is involved in ECM project scope management, and why is good ECM project scope management so important on information technology ECM projects?

80. Do the partners have sufficient financial capacity to keep up the benefits produced by the programme?

81. Is the schedule for the set products being met?

82. What business situation is being addressed?

83. How well defined and documented are the ECM project management processes you chose to use?

84. Is the ECM project making progress in helping to achieve the set results?

85. Is the ECM project supported by national and/or local organizations?

86. Is your organization showing technical capacity and leadership commitment to keep working with the ECM project and to repeat it?

87. To what extent have public/private national resources and/or counterparts been mobilized to contribute to the programs objective and produce results and impacts?

88. In which ECM project management process group is the detailed ECM project budget created?

89. If task x starts two days late, what is the effect on the ECM project end date?

90. On which process should team members spend the most time?

91. Just how important is your work to the overall success of the ECM project?

2.1 Project Management Plan: ECM

92. What data/reports/tools/etc. do your PMs need?

93. Does the selected plan protect privacy?

94. Who manages integration?

95. Are there any windfall benefits that would accrue to the ECM project sponsor or other parties?

96. What went wrong?

97. Has the selected plan been formulated using cost effectiveness and incremental analysis techniques?

98. Do there need to be organizational changes?

99. What are the training needs?

100. Do the proposed changes from the ECM project include any significant risks to safety?

101. How do you manage time?

102. What are the deliverables?

103. What is the business need?

104. What should you drop in order to add something new?

105. Will you add a schedule and diagram?

106. Are cost risk analysis methods applied to develop contingencies for the estimated total ECM project costs?

107. Are there any scope changes proposed for a previously authorized ECM project?

108. Are there any client staffing expectations?

109. What are the assigned resources?

110. If the ECM project management plan is a comprehensive document that guides you in ECM project execution and control, then what should it NOT contain?

111. What would you do differently?

2.2 Scope Management Plan: ECM

112. How do you handle uncertainty or conflict?

113. Are the people assigned to the ECM project sufficiently qualified?

114. Do you have funding for ECM project and product development, implementation and on-going support?

115. Are the proposed ECM project purposes different than the previously authorized ECM project?

116. Are trade-offs between accepting the risk and mitigating the risk identified?

117. Without-plan conditions?

118. For which criterion is it tolerable not to meet the original parameters?

119. Organizational unit (e.g., department, team, or person) who will accept responsibility for satisfactory completion of the item?

120. Are enough systems & user personnel assigned to the ECM project?

121. Have adequate resources been provided by management to ensure ECM project success?

122. Are corrective actions taken when actual results are substantially different from detailed ECM project

plan (variances)?

123. Is there an issues management plan in place?

124. Are all payments made according to the contract(s)?

125. Is your organization structure for both tracking & controlling the budget well defined and assigned to a specific individual?

126. Has stakeholder analysis been conducted, assessing influence on the ECM project and authority levels?

127. Are metrics used to evaluate and manage Vendors?

128. Why is a scope management plan important?

129. Has the budget been baselined?

130. Has a structured approach been used to break work effort into manageable components (WBS)?

131. Has a sponsor been identified?

2.3 Requirements Management Plan: ECM

132. Do you really need to write this document at all?

133. Do you understand the role that each stakeholder will play in the requirements process?

134. Will you perform a Requirements Risk assessment and develop a plan to deal with risks?

135. What performance metrics will be used?

136. Who will perform the analysis?

137. Who is responsible for monitoring and tracking the ECM project requirements?

138. Is requirements work dependent on any other specific ECM project or non-ECM project activities (e.g. funding, approvals, procurement)?

139. Did you avoid subjective, flowery or non-specific statements?

140. After the requirements are gathered and set forth on the requirements register, theyre little more than a laundry list of items. Some may be duplicates, some might conflict with others and some will be too broad or too vague to understand. Describe how the requirements will be analyzed. Who will perform the analysis?

141. Define the help desk model. who will take full responsibility?

142. Are actual resource expenditures versus planned still acceptable?

143. When and how will a requirements baseline be established in this ECM project?

144. How detailed should the ECM project get?

145. Which hardware or software, related to, or as outcome of the ECM project is new to your organization?

146. Is infrastructure setup part of your ECM project?

147. How knowledgeable is the team in the proposed application area?

148. Should you include sub-activities?

149. Does the ECM project have a Change Control process?

150. How will you develop the schedule of requirements activities?

2.4 Requirements Documentation: ECM

151. Are there legal issues?

152. Who is interacting with the system?

153. Is the requirement properly understood?

154. Where do you define what is a customer, what are the attributes of customer?

155. How can you document system requirements?

156. What will be the integration problems?

157. Has requirements gathering uncovered information that would necessitate changes?

158. How will requirements be documented and who signs off on them?

159. The problem with gathering requirements is right there in the word gathering. What images does it conjure?

160. What is your Elevator Speech?

161. How linear / iterative is your Requirements Gathering process (or will it be)?

162. How to document system requirements?

163. What can tools do for us?

164. Where are business rules being captured?

165. Have the benefits identified with the system being identified clearly?

166. How does the proposed ECM project contribute to the overall objectives of your organization?

167. Do your constraints stand?

168. Consistency. are there any requirements conflicts?

169. What facilities must be supported by the system?

170. Is the requirement realistically testable?

2.5 Requirements Traceability Matrix: ECM

171. Do you have a clear understanding of all subcontracts in place?

172. Will you use a Requirements Traceability Matrix?

173. Describe the process for approving requirements so they can be added to the traceability matrix and ECM project work can be performed. Will the ECM project requirements become approved in writing?

174. What percentage of ECM projects are producing traceability matrices between requirements and other work products?

175. How do you manage scope?

176. Why use a WBS?

177. How will it affect the stakeholders personally in their career?

178. What are the chronologies, contingencies, consequences, criteria?

179. How small is small enough?

180. Is there a requirements traceability process in place?

181. Why do you manage scope?

182. What is the WBS?

2.6 Project Scope Statement: ECM

183. Are the meetings set up to have assigned note takers that will add action/issues to the issue list?

184. Elements of scope management that deal with concept development ?

185. Will all ECM project issues be unconditionally tracked through the issue resolution process?

186. Where and how does the team fit within your organization structure?

187. What process would you recommend for creating the ECM project scope statement?

188. Have you been able to thoroughly document the ECM projects assumptions and constraints?

189. Was planning completed before the ECM project was initiated?

190. Will the qa related information be reported regularly as part of the status reporting mechanisms?

191. Are there issues that could affect the existing requirements for the result, service, or product if the scope changes?

192. Elements that deal with providing the detail?

193. Are there backup strategies for key members of the ECM project?

194. If there is an independent oversight contractor, have they signed off on the ECM project Plan?

195. Has the format for tracking and monitoring schedules and costs been defined?

196. How will you haverify the accuracy of the work of the ECM project, and what constitutes acceptance of the deliverables?

197. Will the risk status be reported to management on a regular and frequent basis?

198. Is there a baseline plan against which to measure progress?

199. Write a brief purpose statement for this ECM project. Include a business justification statement. What is the product of this ECM project?

200. Will there be a Change Control Process in place?

201. Who will you recommend approve the change, and when do you recommend the change reviews occur?

202. Has everyone approved the ECM projects scope statement?

2.7 Assumption and Constraint Log: ECM

203. What strengths do you have?

204. How are new requirements or changes to requirements identified?

205. Do you know what your customers expectations are regarding this process?

206. Are there standards for code development?

207. What if failure during recovery?

208. Can you perform this task or activity in a more effective manner?

209. Does a specific action and/or state that is known to violate security policy occur?

210. Has a ECM project Communications Plan been developed?

211. Can the requirements be traced to the appropriate components of the solution, as well as test scripts?

212. If appropriate, is the deliverable content consistent with current ECM project documents and in compliance with the Document Management Plan?

213. When can log be discarded?

214. Contradictory information between document sections?

215. What threats might prevent you from getting there?

216. If it is out of compliance, should the process be amended or should the Plan be amended?

217. Have all necessary approvals been obtained?

218. Does the ECM project have a formal ECM project Plan?

219. Are processes for release management of new development from coding and unit testing, to integration testing, to training, and production defined and followed?

220. What is positive about the current process?

221. Model-building: what data-analytic strategies are useful when building proportional-hazards models?

222. Are there nonconformance issues?

2.8 Work Breakdown Structure: ECM

223. When do you stop?

224. How far down?

225. What is the probability that the ECM project duration will exceed xx weeks?

226. Is it a change in scope?

227. What is the probability of completing the ECM project in less that xx days?

228. How much detail?

229. Can you make it?

230. Why would you develop a Work Breakdown Structure?

231. Why is it useful?

232. How will you and your ECM project team define the ECM projects scope and work breakdown structure?

233. Where does it take place?

234. Who has to do it?

235. When would you develop a Work Breakdown Structure?

236. Is the work breakdown structure (wbs) defined and is the scope of the ECM project clear with assigned deliverable owners?

237. Is it still viable?

238. How big is a work-package?

239. Do you need another level?

240. How many levels?

241. What has to be done?

242. When does it have to be done?

2.9 WBS Dictionary: ECM

243. Are the procedures for identifying indirect costs to incurring organizations, indirect cost pools, and allocating the costs from the pools to the contracts formally documented?

244. The wbs is developed as part of a joint planning session. and how do you know that youhave done this right?

245. Knowledgeable ECM projections of future performance?

246. Are your organizations and items of cost assigned to each pool identified?

247. Do work packages consist of discrete tasks which are adequately described?

248. Intermediate schedules, as required, which provide a logical sequence from the master schedule to the control account level?

249. Does the accounting system provide a basis for auditing records of direct costs chargeable to the contract?

250. Is data disseminated to the contractors management timely, accurate, and usable?

251. Are retroactive changes to direct costs and indirect costs prohibited except for the correction of errors and routine accounting adjustments?

252. Is authorization of budgets in excess of the contract budget base controlled formally and done with the full knowledge and recognition of the procuring activity?

253. Changes in the direct base to which overhead costs are allocated?

254. Are detailed work packages planned as far in advance as practicable?

255. The anticipated business volume?

256. Are internal budgets for authorized, and not priced changes based on the contractors resource plan for accomplishing the work?

257. Are work packages reasonably short in time duration or do they have adequate objective indicators/milestones to minimize subjectivity of the in process work evaluation?

258. Budgets assigned to major functional organizations?

259. Identify and isolate causes of favorable and unfavorable cost and schedule variances?

260. Are overhead cost budgets (or ECM projections) established on a facility-wide basis at least annually for the life of the contract?

2.10 Schedule Management Plan: ECM

261. What is the difference between % Complete and % work?

262. Has a resource management plan been created?

263. What happens if a warning is triggered?

264. Are there any activities or deliverables being added or gold-plated that could be dropped or scaled back without falling short of the original requirement?

265. Timeline and milestones?

266. Is there a formal process for updating the ECM project baseline?

267. Is funded schedule margin reasonable and logically distributed?

268. Identify the amount of schedule variation that triggers a warning. What happens if a warning is triggered?

269. Are the schedule estimates reasonable given the ECM project?

270. Are written status reports provided on a designated frequent basis?

271. Is a pmo (ECM project management office) in

place and provide oversight to the ECM project?

272. Has the ECM project manager been identified?

273. Do all stakeholders know how to access this repository and where to find the ECM project documentation?

274. Does the detailed work plan match the complexity of tasks with the capabilities of personnel?

275. Are the primary and secondary schedule tools defined?

276. Have all documents been archived in a ECM project repository for each release?

277. Have all involved ECM project stakeholders and work groups committed to the ECM project?

278. Staffing Requirements?

279. Quality assurance overheads?

280. Have activity relationships and interdependencies within tasks been adequately identified?

2.11 Activity List: ECM

281. When will the work be performed?

282. When do the individual activities need to start and finish?

283. Is there anything planned that does not need to be here?

284. In what sequence?

285. How difficult will it be to do specific activities on this ECM project?

286. How detailed should a ECM project get?

287. How can the ECM project be displayed graphically to better visualize the activities?

288. Can you determine the activity that must finish, before this activity can start?

289. What are the critical bottleneck activities?

290. What will be performed?

291. What is the LF and LS for each activity?

292. For other activities, how much delay can be tolerated?

293. Where will it be performed?

294. What is the total time required to complete the ECM project if no delays occur?

295. Are the required resources available or need to be acquired?

296. Is infrastructure setup part of your ECM project?

297. How should ongoing costs be monitored to try to keep the ECM project within budget?

298. How much slack is available in the ECM project?

2.12 Activity Attributes: ECM

299. Where else does it apply?

300. Were there other ways you could have organized the data to achieve similar results?

301. How many days do you need to complete the work scope with a limit of X number of resources?

302. Are the required resources available?

303. How much activity detail is required?

304. Is there a trend during the year?

305. How difficult will it be to complete specific activities on this ECM project?

306. What conclusions/generalizations can you draw from this?

307. Which method produces the more accurate cost assignment?

308. What is the general pattern here?

309. What is missing?

310. Resources to accomplish the work?

311. How many resources do you need to complete the work scope within a limit of X number of days?

312. What activity do you think you should spend the most time on?

313. Resource is assigned to?

314. How difficult will it be to do specific activities on this ECM project?

315. Have you identified the Activity Leveling Priority code value on each activity?

2.13 Milestone List: ECM

316. New USPs?

317. Gaps in capabilities?

318. Usps (unique selling points)?

319. Can you derive how soon can the whole ECM project finish?

320. Obstacles faced?

321. It is to be a narrative text providing the crucial aspects of your ECM project proposal answering what, who, how, when and where?

322. Vital contracts and partners?

323. How difficult will it be to do specific activities on this ECM project?

324. Insurmountable weaknesses?

325. Level of the Innovation?

326. What is the market for your technology, product or service?

327. Who will manage the ECM project on a day-to-day basis?

328. Describe the concept of the technology, product or service that will be or has been developed. How

will it be used?

329. What specific improvements did you make to the ECM project proposal since the previous time?

330. Describe your organizations strengths and core competencies. What factors will make your organization succeed?

331. What is your organizations history in doing similar activities?

332. Political effects?

2.14 Network Diagram: ECM

333. What activities must occur simultaneously with this activity?

334. How confident can you be in your milestone dates and the delivery date?

335. Review the logical flow of the network diagram. Take a look at which activities you have first and then sequence the activities. Do they make sense?

336. Exercise: what is the probability that the ECM project duration will exceed xx weeks?

337. How difficult will it be to do specific activities on this ECM project?

338. What are the Major Administrative Issues?

339. Where do schedules come from?

340. What activity must be completed immediately before this activity can start?

341. If x is long, what would be the completion time if you break x into two parallel parts of y weeks and z weeks?

342. Why must you schedule milestones, such as reviews, throughout the ECM project?

343. What is the probability of completing the ECM project in less that xx days?

344. Which type of network diagram allows you to depict four types of dependencies?

345. Are you on time?

346. What must be completed before an activity can be started?

347. If a current contract exists, can you provide the vendor name, contract start, and contract expiration date?

348. Planning: who, how long, what to do?

349. If the ECM project network diagram cannot change and you have extra personnel resources, what is the BEST thing to do?

350. What are the Key Success Factors?

2.15 Activity Resource Requirements: ECM

351. Are there unresolved issues that need to be addressed?

352. How many signatures do you require on a check and does this match what is in your policy and procedures?

353. Organizational Applicability?

354. Time for overtime?

355. Do you use tools like decomposition and rolling-wave planning to produce the activity list and other outputs?

356. What is the Work Plan Standard?

357. When does monitoring begin?

358. Why do you do that?

359. Other support in specific areas?

360. How do you handle petty cash?

361. What are constraints that you might find during the Human Resource Planning process?

362. Anything else?

363. Which logical relationship does the PDM use most often?

2.16 Resource Breakdown Structure: ECM

364. When do they need the information?

365. What is the number one predictor of a groups productivity?

366. Who will be used as a ECM project team member?

367. Which resources should be in the resource pool?

368. Who will use the system?

369. Is predictive resource analysis being done?

370. Why is this important?

371. Who needs what information?

372. Who delivers the information?

373. Why time management?

374. Goals for the ECM project. What is each stakeholders desired outcome for the ECM project?

375. How difficult will it be to do specific activities on this ECM project?

376. Who is allowed to perform which functions?

377. Which resource planning tool provides information on resource responsibility and accountability?

378. What is the purpose of assigning and documenting responsibility?

379. What can you do to improve productivity?

2.17 Activity Duration Estimates: ECM

380. Are contingency plans created to prepare for risk events to occur?

381. What distinguishes one organization from another in this area?

382. Consider the changes in the job market for information technology workers. How does the job market and current state of the economy affect human resource management?

383. Are ECM project records organized, maintained, and assessable by ECM project team members?

384. Is a provider selected based upon defined evaluation criteria?

385. How does a ECM project life cycle differ from a product life cycle?

386. What are the options you found to help people prepare for the exam?

387. How could you define throughput and how would your organization benefit from maximizing it?

388. How much time is required to develop it?

389. Which is the BEST ECM project management tool to use to determine the longest time the ECM project will take?

390. Are ECM project results verified and ECM project documents archived?

391. Does a process exist to determine which risk events to accept and which events to disregard?

392. What are the largest companies that provide information technology outsourcing services?

393. Research recruiting and retention strategies at three different companies. What distinguishes one organization from another in this area?

394. What do you think the real problem was in this case?

395. Are procedures documented for managing risks?

396. Does a process exist to determine the potential loss or gain if risk events occur?

397. Do procedures exist that identify when and how human resources are introduced and removed from the ECM project?

398. What is the career outlook for ECM project managers in information technology?

399. How do functionality, system outputs, performance, reliability, and maintainability requirements affect quality planning?

2.18 Duration Estimating Worksheet: ECM

400. When does your organization expect to be able to complete it?

401. How can the ECM project be displayed graphically to better visualize the activities?

402. What is next?

403. Do any colleagues have experience with your organization and/or RFPs?

404. Value pocket identification & quantification what are value pockets?

405. What is the total time required to complete the ECM project if no delays occur?

406. What utility impacts are there?

407. Is this operation cost effective?

408. What info is needed?

409. Small or large ECM project?

410. What work will be included in the ECM project?

411. Define the work as completely as possible. What work will be included in the ECM project?

412. Can the ECM project be constructed as planned?

413. What questions do you have?

414. How should ongoing costs be monitored to try to keep the ECM project within budget?

415. Why estimate time and cost?

416. What is an Average ECM project?

2.19 Project Schedule: ECM

417. How does a ECM project get to be a year late ?

418. How do you use schedules?

419. Eliminate unnecessary activities. Are there activities that came from a template or previous ECM project that are not applicable on this phase of this ECM project?

420. Did the final product meet or exceed user expectations?

421. Is there a Schedule Management Plan that establishes the criteria and activities for developing, monitoring and controlling the ECM project schedule?

422. How much slack is available in the ECM project?

423. Are you working on the right risks?

424. How do you manage ECM project Risk?

425. How can you shorten the schedule?

426. What is risk?

427. How can you fix it?

428. How effectively were issues able to be resolved without impacting the ECM project Schedule or Budget?

429. Is the structure for tracking the ECM project schedule well defined and assigned to a specific individual?

430. What is risk management?

431. Is infrastructure setup part of your ECM project?

432. Why is software ECM project disaster so common?

433. Why do you need schedules?

434. How detailed should a ECM project get?

435. Change management required?

436. To what degree is do you feel the entire team was committed to the ECM project schedule?

2.20 Cost Management Plan: ECM

437. Are vendor invoices audited for accuracy before payment?

438. Is your organization certified as a broker of the products/supplies?

439. Has a quality assurance plan been developed for the ECM project?

440. Are actuals compared against estimates to analyze and correct variances?

441. Has your organization readiness assessment been conducted?

442. Similar ECM projects?

443. What are the nine areas of expertise?

444. Responsibilities – what is the split of responsibilities between the owner and contractors?

445. Are software metrics formally captured, analyzed and used as a basis for other ECM project estimates?

446. Are meeting objectives identified for each meeting?

447. What does this mean to a cost or scheduler manager?

448. What would you do differently what did not

work?

449. Who will prepare the cost estimates?

450. Is the communication plan being followed?

451. Does the ECM project have a Statement of Work?

452. Are the schedule estimates reasonable given the ECM project?

453. Forecasts – how will the time and resources needed to complete the ECM project be forecast?

454. Have key stakeholders been identified?

2.21 Activity Cost Estimates: ECM

455. What is ECM project cost management?

456. Does the activity use a common approach or business function to deliver its results?

457. Certification of actual expenditures?

458. What were things that you did well, and could improve, and how?

459. What is the last item a ECM project manager must do to finalize ECM project close-out?

460. Who determines when the contractor is paid?

461. When do you enter into PPM?

462. What do you want to know about the stay to know if costs were inappropriately high or low?

463. Was the consultant knowledgeable about the program?

464. What communication items need improvement?

465. Maintenance Reserve?

466. Eac -estimate at completion, what is the total job expected to cost?

467. How and when do you enter into ECM project Procurement Management?

468. What is the ECM projects sustainability strategy that will ensure ECM project results will endure or be sustained?

469. Padding is bad and contingencies are good. what is the difference?

470. Does the activity serve a common type of customer?

471. How do you do activity recasts?

472. Measurable - are the targets measurable?

2.22 Cost Estimating Worksheet: ECM

473. Who is best positioned to know and assist in identifying corresponding factors?

474. Can a trend be established from historical performance data on the selected measure and are the criteria for using trend analysis or forecasting methods met?

475. Is the ECM project responsive to community need?

476. What is the estimated labor cost today based upon this information?

477. What additional ECM project(s) could be initiated as a result of this ECM project?

478. Identify the timeframe necessary to monitor progress and collect data to determine how the selected measure has changed?

479. Will the ECM project collaborate with the local community and leverage resources?

480. What is the purpose of estimating?

481. Ask: are others positioned to know, are others credible, and will others cooperate?

482. What can be included?

483. Is it feasible to establish a control group

arrangement?

484. How will the results be shared and to whom?

485. Does the ECM project provide innovative ways for stakeholders to overcome obstacles or deliver better outcomes?

486. What costs are to be estimated?

487. What happens to any remaining funds not used?

488. What will others want?

2.23 Cost Baseline: ECM

489. What can go wrong?

490. Are you asking management for something as a result of this update?

491. For what purpose ?

492. On time?

493. Does it impact schedule, cost, quality?

494. Does the suggested change request seem to represent a necessary enhancement to the product?

495. Is the cr within ECM project scope?

496. Will the ECM project fail if the change request is not executed?

497. What is your organizations history in doing similar tasks?

498. Should a more thorough impact analysis be conducted?

499. Does a process exist for establishing a cost baseline to measure ECM project performance?

500. What went right?

501. How long are you willing to wait before you find out were late?

502. Definition of done can be traced back to the definitions of what are you providing to the customer in terms of deliverables?

503. Have all approved changes to the schedule baseline been identified and impact on the ECM project documented?

504. How likely is it to go wrong?

505. What do you want to measure ?

506. Has the ECM projected annual cost to operate and maintain the product(s) or service(s) been approved and funded?

507. Are there contingencies or conditions related to the acceptance?

508. Is there anything unique in this ECM projects scope statement that will affect resources?

2.24 Quality Management Plan: ECM

509. Who do you send data to?

510. Does the system design reflect the requirements?

511. What is quality planning ?

512. What is quality and how will you ensure it?

513. Are you meeting the quality standards?

514. How are your organizations compensation and recognition approaches and the performance management system used to reinforce high performance?

515. How do you ensure that your sampling methods and procedures meet your data needs?

516. Is the amount of effort justified by the anticipated value of forming a new process?

517. How are senior leaders, employees, and your organization involved in supporting the community?

518. How do you decide what information needs to be recorded?

519. What else should you do now?

520. Has a ECM project Communications Plan been developed?

521. Do you keep back-up copies of any data?

522. How are deviations from procedures handled?

523. Who needs a qmp?

524. What are your organizations current levels and trends for the already stated measures related to employee wellbeing, satisfaction, and development?

525. Does the ECM project have a formal ECM project Plan?

526. What is the Difference Between a QMP and QAPP?

527. How does your organization maintain a safe and healthy work environment?

528. What changes can you make that will result in improvement?

2.25 Quality Metrics: ECM

529. Is there alignment within your organization on definitions?

530. The metrics–what is being considered?

531. What group is empowered to define quality requirements?

532. When will the Final Guidance will be issued?

533. What method of measurement do you use?

534. What metrics do you measure?

535. Product Availability ?

536. How do you communicate results and findings to upper management?

537. What is the timeline to meet your goal?

538. What forces exist that would cause them to change?

539. Subjective quality component: customer satisfaction, how do you measure it?

540. Has trace of defects been initiated?

541. Is a risk containment plan in place?

542. Are quality metrics defined?

543. What about still open problems?

544. Who notifies stakeholders of normal and abnormal results?

545. Are there already quality metrics available that detect nonlinear embeddings and trends similar to the users perception?

546. What is the benchmark?

547. How are requirements conflicts resolved?

548. When is the security analysis testing complete?

2.26 Process Improvement Plan: ECM

549. Have the frequency of collection and the points in the process where measurements will be made been determined?

550. Have the supporting tools been developed or acquired?

551. Where do you want to be?

552. Everyone agrees on what process improvement is, right?

553. What is the return on investment?

554. If a process improvement framework is being used, which elements will help the problems and goals listed?

555. What personnel are the change agents for your initiative?

556. Where are you now?

557. Modeling current processes is great, and will you ever see a return on that investment?

558. What makes people good SPI coaches?

559. Does your process ensure quality?

560. Are you making progress on the goals?

561. What personnel are the coaches for your initiative?

562. Who should prepare the process improvement action plan?

563. Management commitment at all levels?

564. The motive is determined by asking, Why do you want to achieve this goal?

565. Where do you focus?

566. Purpose of goal: the motive is determined by asking, why do you want to achieve this goal?

567. What personnel are the champions for the initiative?

2.27 Responsibility Assignment Matrix: ECM

568. Do you know how your people are allocated?

569. Competencies and craftsmanship – what competencies are necessary and what level?

570. Contract line items and end items?

571. The total budget for the contract (including estimates for authorized and unpriced work)?

572. Can the contractor substantiate work package and planning package budgets?

573. Where does all this information come from?

574. Does the contractors system identify work accomplishment against the schedule plan?

575. What expertise is not available in your department?

576. If a role has only Signing-off, or only Communicating responsibility and has no Performing, Accountable, or Monitoring responsibility, is it necessary?

577. Who is the ECM project Manager?

578. Direct labor dollars and/or hours?

579. What expertise is available in your department?

580. What simple tool can you use to help identify and prioritize ECM project risks that is very low tech and high touch?

581. Are records maintained to show how management reserves are used?

582. Do others have the time to dedicate to your ECM project?

583. Is accountability placed at the lowest-possible level within the ECM project so that decisions can be made at that level?

2.28 Roles and Responsibilities: ECM

584. Who is responsible for each task?

585. Influence: what areas of organizational decision making are you able to influence when you do not have authority to make the final decision?

586. Is there a training program in place for stakeholders covering expectations, roles and responsibilities and any addition knowledge others need to be good stakeholders?

587. What are your major roles and responsibilities in the area of performance measurement and assessment?

588. What expectations were met?

589. What is working well within your organizations performance management system?

590. How is your work-life balance?

591. Required skills, knowledge, experience?

592. Are ECM project team roles and responsibilities identified and documented?

593. What is working well?

594. Have you ever been a part of this team?

595. Are your budgets supportive of a culture of

quality data?

596. Who is involved?

597. What should you do now to prepare for your career 5+ years from now?

598. What should you highlight for improvement?

599. Key conclusions and recommendations: Are conclusions and recommendations relevant and acceptable?

600. Are governance roles and responsibilities documented?

601. Concern: where are you limited or have no authority, where you can not influence?

602. Do the values and practices inherent in the culture of your organization foster or hinder the process?

2.29 Human Resource Management Plan: ECM

603. Has the ECM project manager been identified?

604. Have stakeholder accountabilities & responsibilities been clearly defined?

605. Is the schedule updated on a periodic basis?

606. Is quality monitored from the perspective of the customers needs and expectations?

607. Are target dates established for each milestone deliverable?

608. Have lessons learned been conducted after each ECM project release?

609. Have the procedures for identifying budget variances been followed?

610. Do people have the competencies to meet the strategic objectives?

611. What did you have to assume to be true to complete the charter?

612. Is documentation created for communication with the suppliers and Vendors?

613. Is there a Steering Committee in place?

614. Based on your ECM project communication management plan, what worked well?

615. How complete is the human resource management plan?

616. Have the key functions and capabilities been defined and assigned to each release or iteration?

617. Does a documented ECM project organizational policy & plan (i.e. governance model) exist?

618. How does the proposed individual meet each requirement?

619. Is there an approved case?

620. Is the steering committee active in ECM project oversight?

621. Are risk oriented checklists used during risk identification?

622. Is there an on-going process in place to monitor ECM project risks?

2.30 Communications Management Plan: ECM

623. How did the term stakeholder originate?

624. How will the person responsible for executing the communication item be notified?

625. What does the stakeholder need from the team?

626. Which stakeholders are thought leaders, influences, or early adopters?

627. Are you constantly rushing from meeting to meeting?

628. Who are the members of the governing body?

629. What are the interrelationships?

630. What is the stakeholders level of authority?

631. Do you feel a register helps?

632. What approaches do you use?

633. What data is going to be required?

634. Do you feel more overwhelmed by stakeholders?

635. Why manage stakeholders?

636. Who have you worked with in past, similar

initiatives?

637. Are others part of the communications management plan?

638. Do you have members of your team responsible for certain stakeholders?

639. Which stakeholders can influence others?

640. Who to learn from?

641. Do you ask; can you recommend others for you to talk with about this initiative?

2.31 Risk Management Plan: ECM

642. Has something like this been done before?

643. How is risk identification performed?

644. What is the cost to the ECM project if it does occur?

645. Minimize cost and financial risk?

646. Number of users of the product?

647. Why do you want risk management?

648. What will the damage be?

649. How much risk can you tolerate?

650. Litigation – what is the probability that lawsuits will cause problems or delays in the ECM project?

651. Are some people working on multiple ECM projects?

652. What risks are tracked?

653. How is implementation of risk actions performed?

654. Do requirements demand the use of new analysis, design, or testing methods?

655. Is this an issue, action item, question or a risk?

656. Risk categories: what are the main categories of risks that should be addressed on this ECM project?

657. What other risks are created by choosing an avoidance strategy?

658. What are some questions that should be addressed in a risk management plan?

659. For software; does the software interface with new or unproven hardware or unproven vendor products?

660. Was an original risk assessment/risk management plan completed?

661. What did not work so well?

2.32 Risk Register: ECM

662. Who is accountable?

663. Preventative actions - planned actions to reduce the likelihood a risk will occur and/or reduce the seriousness should it occur. What should you do now?

664. User involvement: do you have the right users?

665. Are implemented controls working as others should?

666. What has changed since the last period?

667. What can be done about it?

668. Risk categories: what are the main categories of risks that should be addressed on this ECM project?

669. Assume the risk event or situation happens, what would the impact be?

670. Who needs to know about this?

671. Budget and schedule: what are the estimated costs and schedules for performing risk-related activities?

672. What will be done?

673. When would you develop a risk register?

674. Can the likelihood and impact of failing to

achieve corresponding recommendations and action plans be assessed?

675. Manageability – have mitigations to the risk been identified?

676. Have other controls and solutions been implemented in other services which could be applied as an alternative to additional funding?

677. What may happen or not go according to plan?

678. Which key risks have ineffective responses or outstanding improvement actions?

679. What is a Risk?

2.33 Probability and Impact Assessment: ECM

680. What is the level of experience available with your organization?

681. What are the uncertainties associated with the technology selected for the ECM project?

682. Can you stabilize dynamic risk factors?

683. What are its business ethics?

684. How will the consumption pattern change?

685. Sensitivity analysis -which risks will have the most impact on the ECM project?

686. Do you have specific methods that you use for each phase of the process?

687. Does the customer have a solid idea of what is required?

688. Are trained personnel, including supervisors and ECM project managers, available to handle such a large ECM project?

689. What is the ECM project managers level of commitment and professionalism?

690. Is the delay in one subECM project going to affect another?

691. Is the present organizational structure for handling the ECM project sufficient?

692. Do you have a consistent repeatable process that is actually used?

693. Risk categorization -which of your categories has more risk than others?

694. How would you assess the risk management process in the ECM project?

695. Is the number of people on the ECM project team adequate to do the job?

696. Monitoring of the overall ECM project status – are there any changes in the ECM project that can effect and cause new possible risks?

697. What is the past performance of the ECM project manager?

698. Can the ECM project proceed without assuming the risk?

2.34 Probability and Impact Matrix: ECM

699. What are the current or emerging trends of culture?

700. The customer requests a change to the ECM project that would increase the ECM project risk. Which should you do before ass the others?

701. What will be the likely incidence of conflict with neighboring ECM projects?

702. Are there alternative opinions/solutions/ processes you should explore?

703. Are some people working on multiple ECM projects?

704. Can the risk be avoided by choosing a different alternative?

705. How to prioritize risks?

706. Are tool mentors available?

707. Can it be enlarged by drawing people from other areas of your organization?

708. Which is an input to the risk management process?

709. Economic to take on the ECM project?

710. Mitigation -how can you avoid the risk?

711. Premium on reliability of product?

712. Which is the BEST thing to do?

713. Do you use any methods to analyze risks?

714. Pay attention to the quality of the plans: is the content complete, or does it seem to be lacking detail?

715. Is ECM project scope stable?

716. Is the process supported by tools?

717. What are the chances the risk events will occur?

718. Can you avoid altogether some things that might go wrong?

2.35 Risk Data Sheet: ECM

719. What was measured?

720. Who has a vested interest in how you perform as your organization (our stakeholders)?

721. Do effective diagnostic tests exist?

722. What is the chance that it will happen?

723. What actions can be taken to eliminate or remove risk?

724. What are the main threats to your existence?

725. How do you handle product safely?

726. Type of risk identified?

727. What are the main opportunities available to you that you should grab while you can?

728. Will revised controls lead to tolerable risk levels?

729. What do people affected think about the need for, and practicality of preventive measures?

730. How reliable is the data source?

731. Whom do you serve (customers)?

732. How can hazards be reduced?

733. Risk of what?

734. What will be the consequences if it happens?

735. Has a sensitivity analysis been carried out?

736. Has the most cost-effective solution been chosen?

737. What is the likelihood of it happening?

738. What do you know?

2.36 Procurement Management Plan: ECM

739. Is there a Quality Management Plan?

740. Were escalated issues resolved promptly?

741. Is there a procurement management plan in place?

742. Are procurement deliverables arriving on time and to specification?

743. Is there a formal set of procedures supporting Issues Management?

744. Has the ECM project scope been baselined?

745. Are estimating assumptions and constraints captured?

746. Is there a requirements change management processes in place?

747. Are ECM project leaders committed to this ECM project full time?

748. Have lessons learned been conducted after each ECM project release?

749. Are issues raised, assessed, actioned, and resolved in a timely and efficient manner?

750. Is there a set of procedures to capture, analyze and act on quality metrics?

751. Are decisions made in a timely manner?

752. Are assumptions being identified, recorded, analyzed, qualified and closed?

753. Is the ECM project schedule available for all ECM project team members to review?

754. Is the ECM project sponsor clearly communicating the business case or rationale for why this ECM project is needed?

2.37 Source Selection Criteria: ECM

755. How do you consolidate reviews and analysis of evaluators?

756. How long will it take for the purchase cost to be the same as the lease cost?

757. When is it appropriate to conduct a preproposal conference?

758. What are the limitations on pre-competitive range communications?

759. What information is to be provided and when should it be provided?

760. Does the evaluation of any change include an impact analysis; how will the change affect the scope, time, cost, and quality of the goods or services being provided?

761. How do you encourage efficiency and consistency?

762. Do you want to have them collaborate at subfactor level?

763. How do you facilitate evaluation against published criteria?

764. In which phase of the acquisition process cycle does source qualifications reside?

765. What is the last item a ECM project manager must do to finalize ECM project close-out?

766. Are there any common areas of weaknesses or deficiencies in the proposals in the competitive range?

767. Who is entitled to a debriefing?

768. How are oral presentations documented?

769. Is experience evaluated?

770. What should clarifications include?

771. Do proposed hours support content and schedule?

772. What is cost analysis and when should it be performed?

773. Why promote competition?

774. What information may not be provided?

2.38 Stakeholder Management Plan: ECM

775. Have all involved ECM project stakeholders and work groups committed to the ECM project?

776. What other teams / processes would be impacted by changes to the current process, and how?

777. What inspection and testing is to be performed?

778. Have external dependencies been captured in the schedule?

779. Do you use diagrams and tables to account for complex concepts and increase overall readability?

780. What is the process for purchases that arent acceptable (eg damaged goods)?

781. Does the ECM project have a Quality Culture?

782. What proven methodologies and standards will be used to ensure that materials, products, processes and services are fit for purpose?

783. Are milestone deliverables effectively tracked and compared to ECM project plan?

784. Are meeting minutes captured and sent out after the meeting?

785. Does a documented ECM project organizational

policy & plan (i.e. governance model) exist?

786. Contradictory information between different documents?

787. What are the procedures and processes to be followed for purchases, including approval and authorisation requirements?

788. Are enough systems & user personnel assigned to the ECM project?

789. Are the appropriate IT resources adequate to meet planned commitments?

790. Does the resource management plan include a personnel development plan?

791. Where are the verification requirements to be documented (eg purchase order, agreement etc)?

792. Are communication systems proposed compatible with staff skills and experience?

2.39 Change Management Plan: ECM

793. Who in the business it includes?

794. Has the training co-ordinator been provided with the training details and put in place the necessary arrangements?

795. What can you do to minimise misinterpretation and negative perceptions?

796. What prerequisite knowledge or training is required?

797. What risks may occur upfront?

798. Has the training provider been established?

799. What are the responsibilities assigned to each role?

800. Will you need new processes?

801. What type of materials/channels will be available to leverage?

802. What new competencies will be required for the roles?

803. What method and medium would you use to announce a message?

804. What prerequisite knowledge do corresponding groups need?

805. Is it the same for each of the business units?

806. Who will fund the training?

807. What skills, education, knowledge, or work experiences should the resources have for each identified competency?

808. What are the specific target groups/audiences that will be impacted by this change?

809. Have the business unit contacts been selected and notified?

810. Who will do the training?

811. Would you need to tailor a special message for each segment of the audience?

812. Why is it important?

3.0 Executing Process Group: ECM

813. Is the ECM project making progress in helping to achieve the set results?

814. What are the main parts of the scope statement?

815. Have operating capacities been created and/or reinforced in partners?

816. Do ECM project managers understand your organizational context for ECM projects?

817. Are escalated issues resolved promptly?

818. What areas were overlooked on this ECM project?

819. What is the shortest possible time it will take to complete this ECM project?

820. Does the ECM project team have the right skills?

821. How can you use Microsoft ECM project and Excel to assist in ECM project risk management?

822. When is the appropriate time to bring the scorecard to Board meetings?

823. Will new hardware or software be required for servers or client machines?

824. Based on your ECM project communication management plan, what worked well?

825. It under budget or over budget?

826. Mitigate. what will you do to minimize the impact should a risk event occur?

827. If a risk event occurs, what will you do?

828. What are crucial elements of successful ECM project plan execution?

829. Is the program supported by national and/or local organizations?

830. Do schedule issues conflicts?

3.1 Team Member Status Report: ECM

831. Does the product, good, or service already exist within your organization?

832. Are your organizations ECM projects more successful over time?

833. Does every department have to have a ECM project Manager on staff?

834. When a teams productivity and success depend on collaboration and the efficient flow of information, what generally fails them?

835. How much risk is involved?

836. Is there evidence that staff is taking a more professional approach toward management of your organizations ECM projects?

837. Will the staff do training or is that done by a third party?

838. Are the attitudes of staff regarding ECM project work improving?

839. Does your organization have the means (staff, money, contract, etc.) to produce or to acquire the product, good, or service?

840. How does this product, good, or service meet the needs of the ECM project and your organization as a whole?

841. What specific interest groups do you have in place?

842. Are the products of your organizations ECM projects meeting customers objectives?

843. Do you have an Enterprise ECM project Management Office (EPMO)?

844. How it is to be done?

845. The problem with Reward & Recognition Programs is that the truly deserving people all too often get left out. How can you make it practical?

846. How will resource planning be done?

847. What is to be done?

848. How can you make it practical?

849. Why is it to be done?

3.2 Change Request: ECM

850. How are changes graded and who is responsible for the rating?

851. Will new change requests be acknowledged in a timely manner?

852. Are there requirements attributes that can discriminate between high and low reliability?

853. Which requirements attributes affect the risk to reliability the most?

854. Who has responsibility for approving and ranking changes?

855. Who is communicating the change?

856. Describe how modifications, enhancements, defects and/or deficiencies shall be notified (e.g. Problem Reports, Change Requests etc) and managed. Detail warranty and/or maintenance periods?

857. Will the change use memory to the extent that other functions will be not have sufficient memory to operate effectively?

858. How can you ensure that changes have been made properly?

859. Has the change been highlighted and documented in the CSCI?

860. What must be taken into consideration when introducing change control programs?

861. When to submit a change request?

862. Why were your requested changes rejected or not made?

863. Have all related configuration items been properly updated?

864. Are there requirements attributes that are strongly related to the complexity and size?

865. Who can suggest changes?

866. Are change requests logged and managed?

867. How are the measures for carrying out the change established?

868. What are the basic mechanics of the Change Advisory Board (CAB)?

869. What mechanism is used to appraise others of changes that are made?

3.3 Change Log: ECM

870. Where do changes come from?

871. How does this change affect the timeline of the schedule?

872. Is the change request within ECM project scope?

873. Do the described changes impact on the integrity or security of the system?

874. Is the change request open, closed or pending?

875. How does this change affect scope?

876. How does this relate to the standards developed for specific business processes?

877. When was the request submitted?

878. Is this a mandatory replacement?

879. Is the submitted change a new change or a modification of a previously approved change?

880. Is the requested change request a result of changes in other ECM project(s)?

881. Who initiated the change request?

882. Will the ECM project fail if the change request is not executed?

883. Is the change backward compatible without limitations?

884. Does the suggested change request represent a desired enhancement to the products functionality?

885. When was the request approved?

3.4 Decision Log: ECM

886. Linked to original objective?

887. With whom was the decision shared or considered?

888. What was the rationale for the decision?

889. How consolidated and comprehensive a story can you tell by capturing currently available incident data in a central location and through a log of key decisions during an incident?

890. Behaviors; what are guidelines that the team has identified that will assist them with getting the most out of team meetings?

891. Which variables make a critical difference?

892. What is the average size of your matters in an applicable measurement?

893. What eDiscovery problem or issue did your organization set out to fix or make better?

894. How do you know when you are achieving it?

895. What is your overall strategy for quality control / quality assurance procedures?

896. Adversarial environment. is your opponent open to a non-traditional workflow, or will it likely challenge anything you do?

897. Is your opponent open to a non-traditional workflow, or will it likely challenge anything you do?

898. Do strategies and tactics aimed at less than full control reduce the costs of management or simply shift the cost burden?

899. How do you define success?

900. What makes you different or better than others companies selling the same thing?

901. What are the cost implications?

902. Who is the decisionmaker?

903. What alternatives/risks were considered?

904. Who will be given a copy of this document and where will it be kept?

905. At what point in time does loss become unacceptable?

3.5 Quality Audit: ECM

906. Are all staff empowered and encouraged to contribute to ongoing improvement efforts?

907. Quality is about improvement and accountability. The immediate questions that arise out of that statement are: (i) improvement on what, and (ii) accountable to whom?

908. How does your organization know that it is maintaining a conducive staff climate?

909. Is quality audit a prerequisite for program accreditation or program recognition?

910. Is progress against the intentions measurable?

911. Is there a written procedure for receiving materials?

912. How does your organization know that it is effectively and constructively guiding staff through to timely completion of tasks?

913. Will the evidence likely be sufficient and appropriate?

914. Are there appropriate means for intervening if necessary?

915. For each device to be reconditioned, are device specifications, such as appropriate engineering drawings, component specifications and software

specifications, maintained?

916. Statements of intent remain exactly that until they are put into effect. The next step is to deploy the already stated intentions. In other words, do the plans happen in reality?

917. It is inappropriate to seek information about the Audit Panels preliminary views including questions like why do you ask that?

918. How does your organization know that its relationships with other relevant organizations are appropriately effective and constructive?

919. What experience do staff have in the type of work that the audit entails?

920. How does your organization know that its security arrangements are appropriately effective and constructive?

921. Are measuring and test equipment that have been placed out of service suitably identified and excluded from use in any device reconditioning operation?

922. What does an analysis of your organizations staff profile suggest in terms of its planning, and how is this being addressed?

923. Do the suppliers use a formal quality system?

924. Does your organization have set of goals, objectives, strategies and targets that are clearly understood by the Board and staff?

925. How does your organization know that its Governance system is appropriately effective and constructive?

3.6 Team Directory: ECM

926. Process decisions: do invoice amounts match accepted work in place?

927. Who are your stakeholders (customers, sponsors, end users, team members)?

928. What are you going to deliver or accomplish?

929. Who will report ECM project status to all stakeholders?

930. Why is the work necessary?

931. Who are the Team Members?

932. When will you produce deliverables?

933. Where will the product be used and/or delivered or built when appropriate?

934. Decisions: is the most suitable form of contract being used?

935. Decisions: what could be done better to improve the quality of the constructed product?

936. How will the team handle changes?

937. Process decisions: are all start-up, turn over and close out requirements of the contract satisfied?

938. Who will write the meeting minutes and

distribute?

939. How and in what format should information be presented?

940. Do purchase specifications and configurations match requirements?

941. Process decisions: are there any statutory or regulatory issues relevant to the timely execution of work?

942. Contract requirements complied with?

943. Who should receive information (all stakeholders)?

3.7 Team Operating Agreement: ECM

944. Resource allocation: how will individual team members account for time and expenses, and how will this be allocated in the team budget?

945. Reimbursements: how will the team members be reimbursed for expenses and time commitments?

946. Have you established procedures that team members can follow to work effectively together, such as a team operating agreement?

947. What administrative supports will be put in place to support the team and the teams supervisor?

948. Do you post meeting notes and the recording (if used) and notify participants?

949. What are some potential sources of conflict among team members?

950. Are there the right people on your team?

951. Are there influences outside the team that may affect performance, and if so, have you identified and addressed them?

952. What is your unique contribution to your organization?

953. Do you ask participants to close laptops and place mobile devices on silent on the table while the meeting is in progress?

954. Seconds for members to respond?

955. Did you draft the meeting agenda?

956. Did you prepare participants for the next meeting?

957. Is compensation based on team and individual performance?

958. Do team members reside in more than two countries?

959. What is the anticipated procedure (recruitment, solicitation of volunteers, or assignment) for selecting team members?

960. What are the boundaries (organizational or geographic) within which you operate?

961. Do you record meetings for the already stated unable to attend?

962. How do you want to be thought of and known within your organization?

963. Do you send out the agenda and meeting materials in advance?

3.8 Team Performance Assessment: ECM

964. Do you give group members authority to make at least some important decisions?

965. To what degree do team members understand one anothers roles and skills?

966. To what degree do team members agree with the goals, relative importance, and the ways in which achievement will be measured?

967. When a reviewer complains about method variance, what is the essence of the complaint?

968. When does the medium matter?

969. What are you doing specifically to develop the leaders around you?

970. What are teams?

971. To what degree does the teams work approach provide opportunity for members to engage in fact-based problem solving?

972. Social categorization and intergroup behaviour: Does minimal intergroup discrimination make social identity more positive?

973. Where to from here?

974. Do you promptly inform members about major developments that may affect them?

975. To what degree do members understand and articulate the same purpose without relying on ambiguous abstractions?

976. To what degree do team members frequently explore the teams purpose and its implications?

977. To what degree are fresh input and perspectives systematically caught and added (for example, through information and analysis, new members, and senior sponsors)?

978. To what degree will the team ensure that all members equitably share the work essential to the success of the team?

979. How do you encourage members to learn from each other?

980. To what degree are corresponding categories of skills either actually or potentially represented across the membership?

981. To what degree can team members frequently and easily communicate with one another?

982. Effects of crew composition on crew performance: Does the whole equal the sum of its parts?

983. Do friends perform better than acquaintances?

3.9 Team Member Performance Assessment: ECM

984. How are performance measures and associated incentives developed?

985. Does the rater (supervisor) have to wait for the interim or final performance assessment review to tell an employee that the employees performance is unsatisfactory?

986. How are training activities developed from a technical perspective?

987. What makes them effective?

988. Why do performance reviews?

989. How accurately is your plan implemented?

990. To what degree is there a sense that only the team can succeed?

991. What steps have you taken to improve performance?

992. Can your organization rate by exception and assume that most employees are performing at an acceptable level?

993. To what degree is the team cognizant of small wins to be celebrated along the way?

994. How is the timing of assessments organized (e.g., pre/post-test, single point during training, multiple reassessment during training)?

995. What changes do you need to make to align practices with beliefs?

996. How often are assessments to be conducted?

997. What instructional strategies were developed/ incorporated (e.g., direct instruction, indirect instruction, experiential learning, independent study, interactive instruction)?

998. How do you implement Cost Reduction?

999. Which training platform formats (i.e., mobile, virtual, videogame-based) were implemented in your effort(s)?

1000. What are best practices in use for the performance measurement system?

1001. What is the target group for instruction (e.g., individual and collective or small team instruction)?

1002. Are assessment validation activities performed?

1003. What is a general description of the processes under performance measurement and assessment?

3.10 Issue Log: ECM

1004. In your work, how much time is spent on stakeholder identification?

1005. Who is involved as you identify stakeholders?

1006. Are the stakeholders getting the information they need, are they consulted, are concerns addressed?

1007. In classifying stakeholders, which approach to do so are you using?

1008. Can you think of other people who might have concerns or interests?

1009. How were past initiatives successful?

1010. Why do you manage human resources?

1011. What is the impact on the risks?

1012. Do you often overlook a key stakeholder or stakeholder group?

1013. What approaches to you feel are the best ones to use?

1014. How do you manage human resources?

1015. Why do you manage communications?

1016. What help do you and your team need from the

stakeholders?

1017. How often do you engage with stakeholders?

1018. What is a Stakeholder?

1019. Are there common objectives between the team and the stakeholder?

1020. What is the stakeholders political influence?

4.0 Monitoring and Controlling Process Group: ECM

1021. How is agile ECM project management done?

1022. Is progress on outcomes due to your program?

1023. How can you make your needs known?

1024. Is the verbiage used appropriate and understandable?

1025. How well did you do?

1026. Based on your ECM project communication management plan, what worked well?

1027. Who are the ECM project stakeholders?

1028. What resources are necessary?

1029. Where is the Risk in the ECM project?

1030. Purpose: toward what end is the evaluation being conducted?

1031. What departments are involved in its daily operation?

1032. Did it work?

1033. Use: how will they use the information?

1034. What are the goals of the program?

1035. How can you monitor progress?

4.1 Project Performance Report: ECM

1036. To what degree can the cognitive capacity of individuals accommodate the flow of information?

1037. What is the PRS?

1038. To what degree can team members meet frequently enough to accomplish the teams ends?

1039. To what degree are the demands of the task compatible with and converge with the mission and functions of the formal organization?

1040. To what degree do members articulate the goals beyond the team membership?

1041. To what degree does the information network provide individuals with the information they require?

1042. To what degree are the members clear on what they are individually responsible for and what they are jointly responsible for?

1043. To what degree does the informal organization make use of individual resources and meet individual needs?

1044. To what degree does the information network communicate information relevant to the task?

1045. To what degree are the tasks requirements reflected in the flow and storage of information?

1046. To what degree will the approach capitalize on and enhance the skills of all team members in a manner that takes into consideration other demands on members of the team?

1047. To what degree are sub-teams possible or necessary?

1048. To what degree does the teams purpose contain themes that are particularly meaningful and memorable?

1049. To what degree does the formal organization make use of individual resources and meet individual needs?

1050. To what degree is there centralized control of information sharing?

4.2 Variance Analysis: ECM

1051. How does your organization measure performance?

1052. Are all elements of indirect expense identified to overhead cost budgets of ECM projections?

1053. Are records maintained to show how undistributed budgets are controlled?

1054. Are the bases and rates for allocating costs from each indirect pool consistently applied?

1055. Does the contractors system include procedures for measuring the performance of critical subcontractors?

1056. Is the entire contract planned in time-phased control accounts to the extent practicable?

1057. Are indirect costs accumulated for comparison with the corresponding budgets?

1058. Are overhead cost budgets established for each department which has authority to incur overhead costs?

1059. Are the actual costs used for variance analysis reconcilable with data from the accounting system?

1060. Contemplated overhead expenditure for each period based on the best information currently is available?

1061. There are detailed schedules which support control account and work package start and completion dates/events?

1062. Is the anticipated (firm and potential) business base ECM projected in a rational, consistent manner?

1063. What does an unfavorable overhead volume variance mean?

1064. Is cost and schedule performance measurement done in a consistent, systematic manner?

1065. Do you identify potential or actual budget-based and time-based schedule variances?

1066. Does the scheduling system identify in a timely manner the status of work?

1067. What is the total budget for the ECM project (including estimates for authorized and unpriced work)?

1068. Why are standard cost systems used?

1069. Are estimates of costs at completion generated in a rational, consistent manner?

4.3 Earned Value Status: ECM

1070. Where is evidence-based earned value in your organization reported?

1071. How does this compare with other ECM projects?

1072. Verification is a process of ensuring that the developed system satisfies the stakeholders agreements and specifications; Are you building the product right? What do you haverify?

1073. Validation is a process of ensuring that the developed system will actually achieve the stakeholders desired outcomes; Are you building the right product? What do you validate?

1074. If earned value management (EVM) is so good in determining the true status of a ECM project and ECM project its completion, why is it that hardly any one uses it in information systems related ECM projects?

1075. Earned value can be used in almost any ECM project situation and in almost any ECM project environment. it may be used on large ECM projects, medium sized ECM projects, tiny ECM projects (in cut-down form), complex and simple ECM projects and in any market sector. some people, of course, know all about earned value, they have used it for years - but perhaps not as effectively as they could have?

1076. How much is it going to cost by the finish?

1077. Where are your problem areas?

1078. Are you hitting your ECM projects targets?

1079. What is the unit of forecast value?

1080. When is it going to finish?

4.4 Risk Audit: ECM

1081. What is the implication of budget constraint on this process?

1082. When your organization is entering into a major contract, does it seek legal advice?

1083. Have you reviewed your constitution within the last twelve months?

1084. Does willful intent modify risk-based auditing?

1085. Do you have a realistic budget and do you present regular financial reports that identify how you are going against that budget?

1086. Can analytical tests provide evidence that is as strong as evidence from traditional substantive tests?

1087. Are formal technical reviews part of this process?

1088. Do you have an understanding of insurance claims processes?

1089. Is the customer willing to participate in reviews?

1090. Will an appropriate standard of care be applied to all involved?

1091. Have all involved been advised of any obligations they have to sponsors?

1092. Is the customer technically sophisticated in the product area?

1093. Where will the next scandal or adverse media involving your organization come from?

1094. Are testing tools available and suitable?

1095. Are procedures in place to ensure the security of staff and information and compliance with privacy legislation if applicable?

1096. Do you have proper induction processes for all new paid staff and volunteers who have a specific role and responsibility?

1097. Is your organization able to present documentary evidence in support of compliance?

1098. Do you manage the process through use of metrics?

1099. Does the ECM project team have experience with the technology to be implemented?

1100. Have reasonable steps been taken to reduce the risks to acceptable levels?

4.5 Contractor Status Report: ECM

1101. Are there contractual transfer concerns?

1102. What are the minimum and optimal bandwidth requirements for the proposed soluiton?

1103. What was the actual budget or estimated cost for your organizations services?

1104. What process manages the contracts?

1105. What was the budget or estimated cost for your organizations services?

1106. How is risk transferred?

1107. What is the average response time for answering a support call?

1108. Who can list a ECM project as organization experience, your organization or a previous employee of your organization?

1109. What was the final actual cost?

1110. Describe how often regular updates are made to the proposed solution. Are corresponding regular updates included in the standard maintenance plan?

1111. What was the overall budget or estimated cost?

1112. If applicable; describe your standard schedule for new software version releases. Are new software version releases included in the standard maintenance plan?

1113. How long have you been using the services?

4.6 Formal Acceptance: ECM

1114. Have all comments been addressed?

1115. How well did the team follow the methodology?

1116. What lessons were learned about your ECM project management methodology?

1117. Was the ECM project managed well?

1118. Did the ECM project achieve its MOV?

1119. Was the ECM project goal achieved?

1120. Does it do what client said it would?

1121. Do you buy-in installation services?

1122. Is formal acceptance of the ECM project product documented and distributed?

1123. What can you do better next time?

1124. Was the sponsor/customer satisfied?

1125. What is the Acceptance Management Process?

1126. Do you perform formal acceptance or burn-in tests?

1127. General estimate of the costs and times to complete the ECM project?

1128. What function(s) does it fill or meet?

1129. How does your team plan to obtain formal acceptance on your ECM project?

1130. Who supplies data?

1131. What are the requirements against which to test, Who will execute?

1132. Was the client satisfied with the ECM project results?

1133. What features, practices, and processes proved to be strengths or weaknesses?

5.0 Closing Process Group: ECM

1134. Will the ECM project deliverable(s) replace a current asset or group of assets?

1135. What went well?

1136. What will you do to minimize the impact should a risk event occur?

1137. Were risks identified and mitigated?

1138. How will you do it?

1139. How will staff learn how to use the deliverables?

1140. Is the ECM project funded?

1141. When will the ECM project be done?

1142. Did the ECM project management methodology work?

1143. Was the user/client satisfied with the end product?

1144. What is the ECM project Management Process?

1145. What could be done to improve the process?

1146. What will you do?

1147. Can the lesson learned be replicated?

1148. If action is called for, what form should it take?

1149. Is this a follow-on to a previous ECM project?

1150. What were things that you did very well and want to do the same again on the next ECM project?

1151. What is the amount of funding and what ECM project phases are funded?

5.1 Procurement Audit: ECM

1152. Are outsourcing and Public Private Partnerships considered as alternatives to in-house work?

1153. Did the conditions included in the contract protect the risk of non-performance by the supplier and were there no conflicting provisions?

1154. Are there procedures to ensure that changes to purchase orders will be updated on the computer files?

1155. Are idle funds invested, and is interest distributed to the various activity accounts at least annually?

1156. Are review meetings organized during contract execution and do they meet demand?

1157. Does the strategy contain incentives to evaluate the performance of the procurement function/unit?

1158. When competitive dialogue was used, did the contracting authority provide sufficient justification for the use of this procedure and was the contract actually particularly complex?

1159. Are existing suppliers that have a special right to be consulted being contacted?

1160. In a competitive dialogue, were solutions proposed or confidential information given by a candidate not revealed to others without his/her express agreement?

1161. Is the purchasing department organizationally independent of the departments using that function?

1162. Do all requests for materials, supplies, and services require supervisors authorization?

1163. Is the chosen supplier part of your organizations database?

1164. Are requisitions and other purchase requests batched to reduce the number of orders issued?

1165. Is a risk evaluation performed?

1166. Has it been determined which areas of procurement the audit should cover?

1167. Is confidentiality guaranteed during the whole process?

1168. Are incentives to deliver on time and in quantity properly specified?

1169. Does your organization make sources of information beyond the tender documents equally available for all the candidates?

1170. Is the foreseen budget compared with similar ECM projects or procurements yet realised (historical standards)?

1171. If an electronic auction or a dynamic purchasing system was used, did the tender documents specify details on access to information, electronic equipment used and connection specifications?

5.2 Contract Close-Out: ECM

1172. Parties: who is involved?

1173. Was the contract complete without requiring numerous changes and revisions?

1174. Change in attitude or behavior?

1175. Have all contracts been completed?

1176. What happens to the recipient of services?

1177. Parties: Authorized?

1178. Has each contract been audited to verify acceptance and delivery?

1179. How does it work?

1180. Why Outsource?

1181. Change in knowledge?

1182. Have all contract records been included in the ECM project archives?

1183. How is the contracting office notified of the automatic contract close-out?

1184. Change in circumstances?

1185. Have all acceptance criteria been met prior to final payment to contractors?

1186. Was the contract type appropriate?

1187. Was the contract sufficiently clear so as not to result in numerous disputes and misunderstandings?

1188. Are the signers the authorized officials?

1189. What is capture management?

1190. Have all contracts been closed?

1191. How/when used ?

5.3 Project or Phase Close-Out: ECM

1192. Were the outcomes different from the already stated planned?

1193. Planned remaining costs?

1194. What were the desired outcomes?

1195. What could have been improved?

1196. What are they?

1197. What stakeholder group needs, expectations, and interests are being met by the ECM project?

1198. What is this stakeholder expecting?

1199. Planned completion date?

1200. Does the lesson describe a function that would be done differently the next time?

1201. What information did each stakeholder need to contribute to the ECM projects success?

1202. Were cost budgets met?

1203. In addition to assessing whether the ECM project was successful, it is equally critical to analyze why it was or was not fully successful. Are you including this?

1204. Did the delivered product meet the specified

requirements and goals of the ECM project?

1205. Have business partners been involved extensively, and what data was required for them?

1206. Did the ECM project management methodology work?

1207. What is a Risk Management Process?

1208. Who are the ECM project stakeholders and what are roles and involvement?

1209. Who is responsible for award close-out?

5.4 Lessons Learned: ECM

1210. How well did the scope of the ECM project match what was defined in the ECM project Proposal?

1211. How well does the product or service the ECM project produced meet the defined ECM project requirements?

1212. Was ECM project performance validated or challenged?

1213. Were the ECM project objectives met (if not, briefly account for what wasnt met)?

1214. How was the quality of products/processes assured?

1215. How well were expectations met regarding the frequency and content of information that was conveyed to by the ECM project Manager?

1216. How effective was the acceptance management process?

1217. What things surprised you on the ECM project that were not in the plan?

1218. How objective was the collection of data?

1219. What was helpful to know when planning the deployment?

1220. How comprehensive was integration testing?

1221. To what extent was the evolution of risks communicated?

1222. What was the geopolitical history during the origin of your organization and at the time of task input?

1223. How accurately and timely was the Risk Management Log updated or reviewed?

1224. What was the methodology behind successful learning experiences, and how might they be applied to the broader challenge of your organizations knowledge management?

1225. Who needs to learn lessons?

1226. Why does your organization need a lessons learned (LL) capability?

1227. If you had to do this ECM project again, what is the one thing that you would change (related to process, not to technical solutions)?

1228. What skills did you need that were missing on this ECM project?

Index

270